Grammar Dimensions

Book Three
Form, Meaning, and Use

Teacher's Manual

Stephen H. Thewlis

American Language Institute
San Francisco State University

Heinle & Heinle Publishers
A Division of Wadsworth, Inc.
Boston, Massachusetts 02116 U.S.A

Copyright © 1993 by Heinle & Heinle Publishers

All rights reserved. No part of this publication may be reproduced or transmitted in any form or by any means, electronic, or mechanical, including photocopy, recording, or any information storage or retrieval system, without permission in writing from the publisher.

ISBN 0-8384-4129-7

10 9 8 7 6 5 4 3 2

Table of Contents

Introduction to Teacher's Manual —
Grammar Dimensions: Form, Meaning, and Use ... v

Teaching a Sample Unit
**Unit 19: Special Problems with Present Perfect Tense —
Describing Past Events in Relation to the Present** ... viii

Unit 1 • An Overview of the English Verb System 1
Time Frame and Moment of Focus ... 1

Unit 2 • An Overview of the English Verb System 2
Aspect ... 5

Unit 3 • Adverbials ... 10

Unit 4 • Passive Verbs ... 17

Unit 5 • One-Word and Phrasal Modals ... 22

Unit 6 • Infinitives ... 27

Unit 7 • Gerunds ... 33

Unit 8 • Conjunctions ... 38

Unit 9 • Intensifiers ... 42

Unit 10 • Adjective Modifiers ... 45

Unit 11 • Participle Modifiers ... 48

Unit 12 • Comparatives ... 51

Unit 13 • Logical Connectors ... 60

Unit 14 • Degree Complements
Too/Enough...To* and *So/Such...That ... 64

Unit 15 • Factual, Inferential, and Predictive Conditionals — 70

Unit 16 • Adverbials of Purpose and Reason — 76

Unit 17 • Relative Clauses — 78

Unit 18 • Special Problems in Using Present Time
Temporary versus Permanent, Actions versus States — 84

Unit 19 • Special Problems with Present Perfect Tense
Describing Past Events in Relation to the Present — 87

Unit 20 • Special Problems with Future Time
**Using Present Tenses; Using Will versus Going To;
Adverbial Clauses in Future Time** — 90

Unit 21 • Modals of Prediction and Inference — 93

Unit 22 • Hypothetical Statements — 97

Unit 23 • Sensory Verbs — 104

Unit 24 • Causative Verbs — 107

Unit 25 • Articles in Discourse — 111

Unit 26 • Demonstratives in Discourse — 115

Unit 27 • Possessives — 118

Unit 28 • Quantifiers — 122

Unit 29 • Collective Nouns — 127

Unit 30 • Special Problems in Past Time Frame
**Choosing Adverbs versus Aspect Markers
to Indicate Time Relationships** — 130

Unit 31 • Modals in Past Time Frame — 136

Unit 32 • Reported Speech — 142

Introduction to Teacher's Manual — *Grammar Dimensions: Form, Meaning, and Use*

Theoretical Assumptions

Grammar Dimensions rests on a number of assumptions about language and the teaching/learning process. Some of the assumptions are supported by empirical findings; others have been arrived at experientially. In order for the series to be used to best advantage, it is important that the assumptions be made explicit. There are ten:

1. Teachers should be seeking ways of integrating a focus on form or grammar with one on communicative use, rather than on perpetuating the misguided assumption that one must choose between methods that favor one or the other.

2. Grammar does not merely refer to structures or forms. All grammar structures reflect the three dimensions of **form, meaning,** and **use.** For example, the English present progressive consists of some present tense **form** of the verb BE and the present participle, the morpheme *-ing*. The **meaning** the *-ing* ascribes to a verb is that the action/event is in process and, therefore, incomplete. Thus, one of the **uses** of the present progressive is to signal a temporary, as opposed to an enduring, state of affairs (cf. *Peter is living with his parents; Peter lives with his parents*). All three dimensions must be mastered if a student is to be able to use grammar structures **accurately, meaningfully,** and **appropriately.**

3. One of the questions teachers must ask themselves is, "What can I give my students that they can't easily get on their own?" One answer to this question is that I can help draw their attention systematically to the features of the language. They might eventually notice these features on their own, but my calling attention to them will accelerate the process whereby the input to which my students are exposed becomes intake for their acquisition process. Focusing student attention on some aspect of each one of these three dimensions at a time will help my students to develop their own inner criteria for correctness and aid them in the process of self-monitoring.

4. Classroom time is limited. Teachers should not waste time "teaching" students what they already know. Teachers can use student performance as a basis for assessing what it is they need to and are ready to learn.

5. All three dimensions of grammar do not present an equally difficult learning challenge for all learners. Some structures present more of a structural challenge; for others, the long-term challenge is to learn what the structures mean or when to use them. The type and degree of challenge vary according to the inherent complexity of the structure itself and the particular language background and level of English proficiency of the learner. Teachers must continuously ask themselves, "What is the learning challenge of the point I am teaching for this particular group of learners?" They must then devise activities that are likely to afford learning opportunities commensurate with the degree, and appropriate to the type, of challenge.

6. It is likely that there is a sequence of development with regard to learning a language such that learners will not acquire a certain aspect of the target language until they are ready to do so. Teaching does not cause learning. Teachers should not, therefore, expect students to perform perfectly something that has already been introduced. They should, instead, return to the teaching point from time to time, reviewing and expanding upon it.

7. Although grammar is often thought of as an area of language, as opposed to a skill like reading, writing, speaking, or listening, it is in fact a skill. We do not want students simply to know about the language or to be able to recite a rule; we want students to be able to use the grammar. Perhaps we should think of what we do as teaching the skill of "grammaring." As with any skill, mastery takes practice.

8. Learning is enhanced when students are engaged in a variety of purposeful, personally meaningful and enjoyable activities.

9. Students should be led to make generalizations of the highest level possible. For example, rather than learning the present progressive, the past progressive, and the future progressive as individual phenomena, they should learn the general meaning of the *-ing* morpheme as it applies to all three.

10. The acquisition process is not a linear one. Students do not master one structure before going on to tackle another. Moreover, when new structures are introduced, students often backslide with regard to some other aspect of grammar that presumably had already been learned. This may be evidence that the learners' understanding of how English works is being reconfigured. Thus, a temporary lapse in students' performance may actually be evidence of progress.

Distinctive Features of the Series

There are a number of ways these theoretical assumptions about language and the teaching/learning process contribute to the distinctive features of the series.

1. Each unit begins with a communicative **Task.** While engaging in the task, students are using language for communicative or pragmatic purposes. The tasks themselves, however, have been constructed to include instances of the target structure. In this way learners first encounter the target grammar structure in a meaningful context. Thus, the use of communicative tasks provides one way in which grammar and communication can be integrated.

    Another benefit of using tasks is that student performance on the task can be diagnosed by the teacher to determine learning needs. Students may demonstrate that they have already learned what they need to know about a target structure, in which case the unit can be skipped entirely; or it may be possible for the teacher to pinpoint precisely where the students need to work. In this way, teachers can tailor their courses to best meet learner needs and thus contribute to the effective use of limited class time.

2. Relevant facts about the **form, meaning,** and **use** of the target structure are presented in **Focus Boxes** following the task. Student attention can be specifically directed to certain of these focus boxes depending upon the learning challenge for the particular audience of students or the relative importance of the linguistic facts presented. Alternatively, a teacher might choose to work systematically through all the focus boxes in a given unit. Then, too, it is possible for a teacher to decide to work on a portion of a unit and then set it aside to go on to another target structure. Later, the teacher can return to the original unit in a way that allows for review and expansion.

3. Following each focus box is at least one **Exercise** related to the content of the box. The exercises are varied, but every attempt has been made to make them purposeful (e.g., there is no meaningless repetition), personally meaningful (i.e., students are frequently asked to register some opinion or to explain why they chose the answer they did), and enjoyable (thematically coherent and often with "human interest" foci). Besides the exercises in the text, additional exercises can be found in a supplementary workbook which will help give students further practice with "grammaring."

4. At the end of each of the units is a series of **Activities** which help students realize the communicative value of the grammar they are learning. As a complement to the communicative task that opened the unit, grammar and communication are again practice in tandem. Teachers can use student performance on these activities to assess what students have learned and where they still need to work. Teachers should not, however, expect perfect performance at this point.

5. Additional features of the series which address the remaining assumptions are:
   - a **discourse focus** which enables students to generalize at the highest level of language and which helps them learn how to use structures appropriately in context;
   - **free-standing** units which teachers can choose to skip entirely or to sequence in a particular order based upon the unique composition of their class; and
   - a **comprehensive** scope of grammatical structures that spans level of difficulty from beginning to highly advanced, thus meeting the learning needs of learners at all levels of English proficiency.

Diane Larsen-Freeman

Teaching a Sample Unit
Unit 19: Special Problems with Present Perfect Tense — Describing Past Events in Relation to the Present

Background and Rationale

This unit covers an area of the verb tense system which is problematic for most students. Whether or not it is problematic for your class can be determined by doing Units 1 and 2. Those units provide an overview of the verb system, and a wide variety of exercises and activities that can be used to diagnose whether additional study and practice are necessary. Alternatively, you can use the Task or one of the Activities in this unit as a diagnostic exercise.

Most intermediate students have good control over the forms of the present perfect and present perfect progressive tenses, but cannot correctly interpret the meanings implied by these forms, nor can they use them appropriately. In particular, they are puzzled by situations when both present perfect and simple past tense may be grammatically correct, and choosing one form instead of another indicates a subtle meaning difference. The focus of this chapter is on meaning and use: to help students develop an understanding of the notion of "present relevance" or "relationship to the present."

Task

ALTERNATIVES TO THE TASK

Some of the topics for writing and discussion activities in this book were developed for use with university-bound students and reflect their interests and priorities. But most activities deal with topics that can easily be used with all kinds of students. The Task in this unit is an example of one such "academic" topic that may not be appropriate for your specific class. If your students are not preparing for academic study in a college or university, you may wish to use one of the Activities instead. They are discussed in detail below. The rationale for choosing one activity instead of another depends on what you want to focus on, and what the students have done previously.

For example, Activity 1 calls for the same kind of essay as the Task, but with a more generalized topic. Activity 2 resembles somewhat the Task in Unit 3, in which newspaper articles are used to give students a chance to look at the information content of news stories in order to review *wh-questions* and distinguish the subject–predicate core of a sentence from additional adverbial information. Accordingly, if your students have recently done that Task, you might choose to do this activity as a follow-up (if you feel that the students enjoyed working with newspaper articles) or avoid the activity (if you feel that the activity might seem too similar to the previous one).

Alternatively, you may wish to substitute Activity 3 or 4, which both focus much more on oral production, and give students an opportunity for structured interviews with both classmates and people outside of class. Almost every unit has a number of topics concerning cross-cultural differences (such as Activity 5) that can be used for small-group or whole-class discussions. The topics have proven to be of great interest to most students. You will need to decide whether you want to stress the "grammar focus" in such activities, or the "content focus," and adjust your emphasis accordingly. All the activities can be used to diagnose problems with present perfect by asking students to write responses for you to examine.

DOING THE TASK

The Task is designed to provide an example of a situation in which correct use of present perfect would be extremely important. It is also a task that many of your students will probably need to do in the "real world," and so it gives an opportunity for them to practice. The application form and subsequent steps in idea-generation comprise important prewriting activities that will help your students write an appropriate essay. There are many ways to do the Task. You may wish to begin by asking students about their post-English class academic plans, and asking what steps they have taken. Depending on your situation, you could follow up the Task by working with your students on their own actual college applications. You can lead the class as a whole through the development of their list of characteristics in a step-by-step fashion, or go over the whole process as written and let them work together in pairs or groups. Students from some countries will find this topic very challenging, while others will have no trouble thinking of things that make them different from other people. Some students feel more secure working with a model. Since the focus of this book is grammar, not process-writing, a model has been provided in Exercise 1. If, however, your students don't need a model, or you prefer a process-approach that doesn't use one, feel free to disregard it.

You can shorten the Task but still keep its diagnostic potential by having the students hand in their statements of "formative experiences" and the "resulting achievements," and skipping the step of writing a full essay. This will give you information on students' control of form. If you want to check students' understanding of the meaning and use components of present perfect, having the students write a paragraph or brief essay will provide much more complete and reliable information.

Focus 1

There are many ways to present the information in a Focus box. How you do it will depend on your class, your own preferred teaching style, the time available to cover the material, and concerns for variety in approach. In this Focus box, you can:

- assign students to read the Focus box before class and ask if they have any questions about the material.
- present the information orally and then have students look at the example sentences. (Example sentences have been marked in the order in which they are likely to be presented or studied, but you may wish to change that order.)
- write the example sentences on the board (or similar sentences that refer to real students and events in your class: "Maria **applied** to three universities, and she **got accepted** to all of them" versus "Maria **has applied** to three universities, but she **still hasn't gotten** a reply from them") and ask students why different tenses have been used.
- put students into pairs or small groups and have them compare the Present Time Frame and Past Time Frame counterparts. Group One will look at example sentences (a) and (b), Group Two will look at (c) and (d), and so forth. Students can examine the sentences and formulate a rule for when they should use past tense and when they should use present perfect tense. Each group or pair presents their rule or explanation to the rest of the class.
- have students read the explanation in the book as a follow-up at the end of the presentation, or as homework for review.
- combine Focus 1 and 2 in a teacher-presented explanation.

You will undoubtedly want to use a variety of presentation techniques to keep the students interested and involved.

Exercise 1

This is an example of an **open-ended exercise.** There are many such exercises in the book. They provide students with an opportunity to recognize, identify, and classify structures, and to form and test hypotheses about the meaning and use of those structures in longer texts. The point of an open-ended exercise is to get students to **observe, discuss,** and **explain** the form, meaning, and use dimensions of various structures. In most open-ended exercises, there is often no **single** definitive right answer, and the **process** of hypothesis-forming and -testing is the real point of the exercise. This is a very different kind of exercise than most students (and many teachers) may be used to, but current research supports giving students opportunities to analyze and formulate explanations of grammatical phenomena. Such activities encourage students to become independent gatherers of grammatical data and active hypothesizers, and to extend these skills to language situations outside the classroom.

DOING OPEN-ENDED EXERCISES

The approach to all the open-ended exercises in this book is basically the same. The first step is to have students read the passage for understanding. For shorter passages, this can be done in class, but for longer ones it is probably better to have the students read them as homework. This particular text was designed to also be used in connection with the Task, so students will probably have already done this step. But if they haven't read it previously, you may want to follow-up to the presentation of Focus 1 with Exercise 2, and come back to Exercise 1 the next day, after students have read the passage as homework. In every unit, there are several different exercise types — ranging from highly structured to very open-ended — so you shouldn't worry about omitting some, or rearranging the order that you do them.

The next step (marked *1* in the instructions for this particular open-ended exercise) is to make sure that students can correctly recognize the structures being focused on, and, in this case, to identify both their form and their meaning. This step can also be assigned as homework, or done in pairs in class.

There are as many ways to correct this step as there are to present Focus boxes, depending on how much class time is available to go over the exercise, what kinds of other activities the students have just been doing, and what you want to emphasize. You can check how well students have done the identification and classification part of these open-ended exercises:

- by going over the passage together, calling on students individually. (What's the first verb you underlined? How did you mark it? What's the next verb you identified?)
- by having students compare their marked texts with those of another student.
- by having students exchange books and correct each other's work, based on the class discussion.
- by providing the answers yourself, and asking the students if they have questions.

Your preferred method will vary from class to class and from day to day. Giving students a variety of activities and an opportunity to develop good self-monitoring skills should guide your choices.

The next step (marked *2* in this exercise) is the real "open-ended" part of such exercises. Students can work in pairs, small groups, or in a teacher-led discussion. Students should be encouraged to apply what they have already learned to explain the "why" of tense use. The questions asked in this part of an open-ended exercise usually function as "topics for discussion" rather than questions demanding a single definitive "right" answer. In many (but not all) of these exercises, a single possible explanation or a "most likely" interpretation (based on native speaker responses) has been indicated in the Answer Key, but no feasible opinion should be discounted. Giving students an opportunity to defend their answers encourages them to form their own hypotheses about grammar and to test those hypotheses through continued observation and analysis. This particular exercise represents a good opportunity to review, as well as to recycle the information on when and why authors change Time Frame within a text.

Focus 2

This is a "pivot" focus. It can be combined with a presentation of Focus 1. Alternatively, you can combine it with, or present it in explicit contrast to, Focus 3 and Focus 4. Various ways to present the information have been suggested above.

Exercise 2

This book provides many different learning and practice activities that are appropriate to all kinds of methodological approaches and teaching styles. This is a more **"traditional" exercise** of the sort that appear in most grammar books. "Fill in the blanks," "choose the correct form," "transform the sentence" are all examples of these kinds of "traditional" exercises. Most of these exercises have been designed so that they can be done either orally in class, or assigned as written homework to be handed in. They can be used as **practice** activities, in which students gain understanding and mastery by doing the exercise; or they can be used as **testing** activities, in which student performance on the exercise will give you an idea of how well they understand the teaching point, and whether or not further review and practice are necessary. How you choose to do them will depend on your class and where the exercise fits in with the ongoing sequence of activities.

Most teachers and students are familiar with these kinds of exercises, and feel comfortable doing them. But the "traditional" exercises in this book have an important difference: In many cases, there is more than one right answer. This is intentional, since students at this level need to be able to choose from a number of **possible** grammatically correct forms and decide on the **most appropriate** form for a specific situation. There are rather few *either/or* choices at this level. Such multiple-right-answer exercises will also help students develop the habit of actively verifying their own choices, and explaining why they have chosen a particular answer. Multiple right answers mean that any answer that is different from the teacher's answer could also be potentially correct. So students need to verify alternative possibilities, and learn to distinguish answers that are ungrammatical from answers that are grammatical but have a different meaning or use.

DOING "TRADITIONAL" EXERCISES

There are many ways to do an exercise, depending on what other additional "grammar acquisition skills" you might want to emphasize. For example, you may want to give students a chance to develop careful self-monitoring skills, in which case, you may want to evaluate how accurately a student has corrected his or her own work. You may want to give your students a chance to work on making and verifying their hypotheses, in which case having students compare and "defend" their answers might be a good way to go over a particular exercise. Like everything else, you will want to vary what you do with these exercises so that students don't become bored with one single approach. Here are some of the ways you can do these kinds of "traditional" exercises:

- You can use them as "testing" or diagnostic activities, such as an in-class quiz, where students write individual answers which are corrected by the teacher, by peers, or by the student.

- You can use them as learning activities in which students work together in pairs and compare their answers with each other.

- You can use them as practice activities by doing them aloud as a whole class, calling on individual students for specific answers.

- They can be done in written form as homework or orally in class.

- In order to encourage students to ask questions and verify their own answers, you can give students "your" answers. Students with different answers should be reminded that if their answer is different from yours, it could be either right or wrong — it is **their** responsibility to find out which by asking the teacher.

- You can have students correct each other's homework, and then you can evaluate the accuracy of the corrector's work/judgment.

- If you have limited class time and want to spend it on more "communicative" practice, you can skip the exercise entirely and go on to Exercise 3.

Focus 3

Various different presentation techniques were described in Focus 1. They can be used with this Focus box as well, or you may wish to combine a couple of different ways. For example, here you can paraphrase the information contained in the Focus box ("Here are three situations in which we usually use present perfect..."), then have the students discuss the example sentences (or similar sentences of your own) in your preferred way, and then finally assign the actual Focus box for the students to read at home as review.

Exercise 3

There are many exercises in the book that are designed to provide **structured conversation practice** using specific grammatical patterns. Some teachers prefer to use these in lieu of "traditional" exercises, while others use them as a follow-up activity to such exercises.

DOING STRUCTURED CONVERSATION PRACTICE EXERCISES

There are a number of possible ways to do these kinds of exercises:

- These exercises are obviously most logically done as paired oral exercises, with a report to the rest of the class to check for accurate use of the structures.

- You can stress the practice potential of the exercise by just giving students an opportunity to talk, without making a report.

- You can easily adapt such exercises to include writing practice, or to be used as a communicative testing exercise, by having your students write their questions and having their partners respond in writing. Alternatively, you can use the structured communication exercise to serve as the basis for a written report about the partner that will be handed in for correction or grading.

- Evaluating the content as well as the form (Who has the most interesting or unusual questions?) is a good way to ensure that students correctly understand the meaning and use dimensions of various forms.

Exercise 4

This "traditional" exercise calls for students to choose one of only two possible forms. You may want to vary the exercise for more advanced students by allowing them to choose **any** correct form, and to explain why they feel their choice is correct.

Focus 5

This is the most problematic area for students to understand: The connection between the present can be stated, implied, or "none of the above." This might be a good Focus box to assign for individual study the night before, and then go over it as a class the next day in connection with Exercises 5 and 6.

Exercise 5

Many students find this exercise extremely difficult, because both answers are grammatically possible, but one is preferred. Students should be reminded that questions of grammar at this level are rarely *either/or* propositions. In fact, many choices are made because of the context of a particular sentence — discourse issues — not a simple selection of a form. In this exercise, the most logical continuation is usually the sentence which is in the same time frame as the cue sentence.

Exercise 6

This is an example of an open-ended exercise with short passages (rather than a longer text). Like other exercises, there are many possible variations:

- It can be done in pairs, small groups, or by the whole class together with you leading the discussion.

- You can have your students prepare it as homework and then explain their ideas in class, or you can have students do the initial reading and analysis in class, since the passages are short.

- You may decide to do one or two with the whole class, as an example, and then assign the others to be done in pairs. You can shorten the exercise by assigning only one or two sentences to each pair or group.

- Or you may wish to use the exercise in connection with Focus 5, as a source of additional examples of the logical relationships to the present that are described in the Focus box.

Focus 6

This Focus is a good example of how you will want to vary your approach to Focus boxes, depending on what has already occurred in the class. The information is a recycling of the material on contrasts in meaning that are communicated by aspect (discussed in Unit 2). If you are doing this unit as a follow-up to the overview of the verb system, you may not need to present these contrasts again, but just use the example sentences to review those concepts. If you are doing this unit later in the semester, this Focus box presents a good opportunity to recycle and review more explicitly some of the basic aspectual distinctions that we make in English.

Exercises 7 and 8

These "traditional" exercises have a different scope and purpose, and so they should be done in different ways. Exercise 7 focuses on the distinctions in meaning communicated by present perfect progressive rather than present perfect. Exercise 8 is a summary exercise of all the points in the unit. Exercise 7 would most logically be done as a follow-up to the Focus box — orally, in class. Exercise 8, while it could be done the same way, would probably be more useful as a quiz or assigned as homework, and corrected with any of the processes described in the comments on Exercise 2.

Activities

As suggested in the section on the Task, Activities can be used in place of Tasks and vice versa. Most units end with some "summary" exercises that can be used to test students' understanding, but the Activities are probably better at providing a productive and holistic evaluation of the students' mastery of the material.

ACTIVITY 1

The "report to the class" can be either written or oral. If you decide to use the activity as an essay topic, you may want to remind the students that the purpose of the exercise is to **use** the structures they have been studying in real situations, so they should try to use them in their writing wherever possible. An extremely useful way to correct these essays is by highlighting problems with verb tense choice in the students' papers, and returning them for the students to correct.

ACTIVITY 2

This is really another kind of "open-ended" opportunity for discussion like those provided in Part 2 of Exercise 1 and Exercise 6, except students bring in their own texts for analysis and discussion. You can do it as written, or, alternatively, you may want to pick out articles yourself, to make sure that there are useful examples for students to look at. You may want different groups to look at different articles or all groups to examine the same one. The "presentation to the rest of the class" can be a formal presentation or a general teacher-led discussion with the whole class.

ACTIVITY 3

The focus is a structured interview situation. Like Activity 2, the "report to the rest of the class" can be a formal presentation by a member of the group or a general class discussion. Alternatively, you can have students report the answers of individual students in written full-sentence form. *(Maria has quit smoking recently. Lately she has been getting worried about her health. Quitting smoking has made her more nervous, and she has gained some weight.)* These sentences can be used for testing or diagnosis, or corrected in the manner described in the comments on Activity 1.

ACTIVITIES 4 AND 5

Sometimes Activities in this book have a logical link and can fruitfully be combined into a larger task. Units 4 and 5 are good examples of this. Activity 4 can be used as an in-class "rehearsal" for an out-of-class contact assignment to interview Americans. The subsequent discussion can be done in small groups, or, less formally, by the class as a whole. If you are teaching in a program in which students have a number of different classes (grammar, conversation class, American culture class), activities that you don't teach yourself may be done in another class. These activities could fit easily into conversation class or an oral communication or cross-cultural communication class as well.

Final Thoughts

These materials have been designed to help students become independent acquirers of grammatical competence. They capitalize on (and help students continue to develop) their abilities of observation, analysis, and hypothesis-formation, -testing, and -refinement. They have been designed to provide students with an extremely wide variety of activities, ranging from "traditional" transformation drills to open-ended discussion topics and out-of-class contact assignments. But above all, the exercises have been designed to be **easily adaptable.** You should always look upon the directions in the book as **"suggestions"** for use, and never hesitate to adapt any particular exercise for your own purposes. In this sample unit, I have attempted to show some of the ways that are readily at your disposal. Variety seems to be an important ingredient for establishing and maintaining student interest, engagement, and motivation.

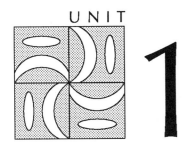

UNIT 1

An Overview of the English Verb System 1

Time Frame and Moment of Focus

Task

Use the Task as a diagnostic for students' command of verb forms and their uses. Typically, students at this level have good formal control of the verb tenses, but poorly developed notions of subtle differences in meaning conveyed by different tenses, and the common uses of tenses in extended discourse. Units 1 and 2 are designed to give students an overall review of forms, and a consolidated understanding of the basic patterns of tense meaning and use. Individual contrasts are additionally practiced in other units of this text (in particular, Units 18, 19, and 30, and Unit 20, Focus 6). These first two units can be used to determine whether your students need explicit additional practice for tense contrasts within single time frames.

Exercise 1

1. Past 2. Present 3. Past 4. Future (Draw attention to the fact that present tense forms are used in Future Time Frame.) 5. Past 6. Present 7. Present

Exercise 2

1. (a) *had* — simple past (b) *was* — simple past; *were burning* — past progressive (c) *had been sneezing* — past perfect progressive (d) *hated* — simple past (e) *meant* — simple past; *meant* — simple past

2. (a) *don't know* — simple present (b) *starts* — simple present (c) *I'm trying* — present progressive (d) *I've been* — present perfect (e) *It's* — simple present (f) *I've been working* — present perfect progressive; *need* — simple present (g) *I've saved* — present perfect (h) *can't decide* — simple present (modal auxiliary)

3. (a) *were* — simple past (b) *had been* — past perfect (c) *had known* — past perfect; *decided* — simple past

4. (a) *will mean* — simple future (b) *think* — simple present; *will become* — simple future; *are* — simple present (c) *require* — simple present; *will be* — simple future (d) *will have to develop* — simple future (phrasal modal auxiliary); *may not be* — simple future (e) *may have become* — future perfect

5. (a) *was* — simple past (b) *compared* — simple past (c) *was* — simple past (d) *were* — simple past; *were dying out* — past progressive; *had lost* — past perfect

6. (a) *has* — simple present (c) *have discovered* — present perfect; *can prevent* — simple present (d) *have been established* — present perfect (passive); *provide* — simple present

7. (a) *are developing* — present progressive (b) *result* — simple present (c) *are proving* — present progressive (d) *worry* — simple present (e) *have apparently helped* — present perfect

Exercise 3

1. From the sentences that refer to **Present Time,** examples of verb phrases used to express:
   a. a timeless truth — 6: a, c (can prevent); 7: b, d

b. a past event or situation that is related to the present — 2: d, f (*been working*), g; 6: c (*have discovered*), d (*have been established*); 7: e
   c. an action still in progress — 2: c, f (*been working*); 7: a, c
   d. a general relationship — 2: e, f (*need*)
   e. a state that is true now: 2: a, f (*need*), h
2. From the sentences that refer to **Future Time,** examples of verb phrases used to express:
   a. an event that is already scheduled to take place in the future — 2: b
   b. an event or state that is predicted for the future — 4: a, b (*will become*), c (*will be*), d, e
   c. an event that will take place up until and including a specific future time — 4: e
3. From the sentences that refer to **Past Time,** examples of verb phrases used to express:
   a. a general statement — 1: d, e; 3: a; 5: a, b, c, d
   b. a continuous or repeated action that happened in the past — 1: c; 5: d
   c. an action or state that took place before other events in the past — 1: c; 3: b, c (*had known*); 5: d (*had lost*)
   d. an action that took place at a specific time in the past — 1: a, b; 3: c (*decided*)

Exercises 4, 5, and **6** can be combined into a single open-ended exercise:

Exercise 4

1. My brother <u>called</u> me <u>up</u> yesterday. [simple past] / I always <u>know</u> he <u>needs</u> to borrow money when he <u>calls</u>, because I [general truth / simple present / simple present] never <u>hear</u> from him at any other time. [simple present / movement to specific example] / We <u>spoke</u> about this and that for a few minutes. He <u>asked</u> about my [simple past / simple past] job and my family. We <u>talked</u> about his problems with his boss. [simple past] / These <u>are</u> typical topics before he finally [general truth / simple present] <u>asks</u> for a loan. [simple pres. / movement to spec. ex.] / This phone call <u>was</u> no exception. He <u>needed</u> $50 "until payday." [simple past / simple past] / Somehow, when payday <u>comes</u> he never <u>remembers</u> to pay back the loan. [simple present / simple present]

2. I<u>'ll be</u> really happy when the summer <u>is</u> over. [simple future / simple present general truth] / I <u>don't like</u> hot weather, and I <u>can't stand</u> mosquitoes. [simple present / simple present] There<u>'s</u> a lot of both of those things in the summer. [simple present] / Last summer I <u>tried</u> to escape by going on a trip to [clear time marker, specific example / simple past] Alaska. The heat <u>wasn't</u> bad, but the mosquitoes <u>were</u> terrible! [simple past / simple past] / Next year I <u>think</u> I<u>'ll consider</u> a vacation in [clear time marker / simple present / simple future] Tierra del Fuego. / I <u>understand</u> it<u>'s</u> really cold there in July. [simple present / general truth]

3. For more than 50 years, scientists around the world <u>have used</u> a single means of measuring the strength (or [present perfect / movement from general statement to specific example] magnitude) of earthquakes. / The Richter scale <u>was developed</u> by Charles Richter in 1935. It <u>was designed</u> [simple past (passive) / simple past (passive)] so scientists <u>could compare</u> the intensity of earthquakes in different parts of the world. It <u>was designed</u> to [simple past with modal auxiliary / simple past (passive)] measure intensity in earthquakes, not damage. / This <u>is</u> because a less powerful earthquake in a heavily [statement of general truth / simple present] populated area <u>can cause</u> more damage than a stronger earthquake in an unpopulated area. [simple present]

4. Every year archaeologists and anthropologists <u>find</u> [simple present] out more information about how the Western Hemisphere <u>was settled</u> [simple past (passive)]. By examining burial sites and learning about the linguistic relationships between various languages, researchers <u>have established</u> [present perfect] some basic facts about how and when man first <u>came</u> [simple past] to the New World. [focus changes from archaeologists to Indians] / Native Americans (or "Indians," as they <u>came</u> [simple past] to be known) <u>inhabited</u> [simple past] North America in several "waves" of migration. The first wave <u>was</u> [simple past] at least 15,000 years ago. The most recent wave probably <u>ended</u> [simple past] with the retreat of the glaciers at the end of the last Ice Age. [focus returns to archaeologists/experts] / Although there <u>is</u> [simple present] still disagreement among experts as to exactly when and how many "waves" actually <u>occurred</u> [simple past], most researchers <u>agree</u> [simple present] that there <u>were</u> [simple past] at least three and perhaps as many as five separate migrations.

Exercise 5

Passage #4 has several "internal" time changes. There are two basic time frames in this passage: when the New World was settled and when archaeologists discovered this information. Students should be able to distinguish the general shift in focus from one period to the other, and the attendant "basic tense" of those sentences.

Exercise 6

You may wish to omit this exercise if students are not having trouble identifying verb phrases in connected discourse or identifying the correct name of the tense.

Exercise 7

This is an open-ended exercise.

1. Moment of focus: "when I saw someone"; explicitly stated; point of time: saw/period of time: yesterday afternoon
2. Moment of focus: "The moment Peter heard that John F. Kennedy had been assassinated"; explicitly stated; point of time
3. Moment of focus: "Rome was badly damaged"; explicitly stated; point of time: "was damaged"/period of time: "during the first century A.D."
   Moment of focus: (after the fire) "It was widely believed…"; implied; period of time
4. Moment of focus: "the last years of Mozart's life"; explicitly stated; period of time
5. Moment of focus: "When John first arrives in Paris"; explicitly stated; point of time
   Moment of focus: "Once he is able to speak enough French"; explicitly stated; point of time
6. Moment of focus: "the party"; implied; period of time

Exercise 8

You may choose to omit this exercise if students are not having trouble identifying verb phrases. You may wish to point out the passive and modal auxiliaries as a preview/diagnostic of other units in the book.

1. I <u>had</u> an interesting experience yesterday afternoon. I <u>was walking</u> from my house to the grocery store when I <u>saw</u> someone I <u>had gone</u> to high school with.
2. The moment Peter <u>heard</u> that John F. Kennedy <u>had been assassinated was</u> one that he <u>would never forget</u>. He <u>was</u> a junior in high school. He <u>was studying</u> in the school library at the time.
3. The Imperial City of Rome <u>was</u> badly damaged by fire during the first century A.D. It <u>was widely believed</u> that the Emperor Nero <u>played</u> a violin while the city <u>burned</u> to the ground.
4. During the last years of his life, Wolfgang Amadeus Mozart <u>was</u> virtually penniless. In spite of his fame as a composer, he <u>was forced</u> to borrow from friends, and to move frequently, since he <u>was</u> unable to pay his rent.
5. When John first <u>arrives in</u> Paris, he<u>'s going to stay</u> with a local French teacher and his family. Once he <u>is able to speak</u> French well enough, he <u>will probably find</u> a small apartment of his own.
6. What <u>will you bring</u> to the party? I <u>hear</u> we<u>'ll be playing</u> games. I <u>hope</u> there <u>will be</u> dancing as well!

Activities

Activity 1

This Activity can be used in place of the Task if you want to focus on giving students an opportunity to talk about their own lives, or start on introductions.

Activity 2

The first two steps of this Activity can be done either as written homework or paired interviews. The third step can be omitted if you wish to use this activity as additional sentence construction practice.

Alternatively, all three steps can be combined into one written activity, to be used to check mastery of Present and Past Time verb tenses. Incorrect tense choice in the third part (what things have changed the most) can be an indication that the students may need additional work with Unit 19 (past events with a relation to the present).

Activity 3

This activity practices tense use in Future Time, and Past events with a relation to the present, and tenses in Past Time. It can be done in written form, in small groups, or as a question/answer oral exercise.

Activity 4

Students can present the articles to the rest of the class, or turn them in to the teacher with the examples highlighted or underlined.

Activity 5

This activity has a dual purpose. First, students get practice in making statements about their language ability in all three time frames. An **equally important** part of this activity is the opportunity it affords for students to do a self-evaluation, set some personal goals, and identify some possible strategies for achieving those goals. For more advanced classes, this activity may be used as an initial activity at the very beginning of the course.

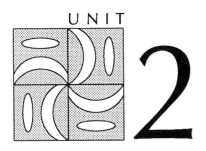

UNIT 2

An Overview of the English Verb System 2
Aspect

Task

This can be done as pair work or as a written diagnostic. There should be at least three sentences to describe each picture. For example:

> There has been an earthquake, because things are lying all over the floor. People are picking up the things that aren't broken, and putting them back on the shelves. There will probably be an aftershock, because that's often what happens in earthquakes.

The Task can be used as a diagnostic for student use of perfect and progressive aspect. If necessary, explicit practice in present, future, and past time frames are provided in Units 18, 19, 20, and 30.

Exercise 1

This is an open-ended exercise. Some information has been provided to help you process and guide the discussion. Answers for the first paragraph also indicate aspect. Answers for the third paragraph indicate some of the basic uses of simple aspect.

1. By the time <u>John gets on Flight 53 to Paris</u> the day after tomorrow, he <u>will have accomplished</u> [before/perfect aspect] a great deal in a relatively short period of time. He <u>will have moved out</u> [before/perfect aspect] of the apartment where he <u>has been living</u> [before/perfect progressive aspect] for the last couple of years. He <u>will have said</u> [before/perfect aspect] some long, sad good-byes. He <u>will certainly be thinking</u> [at the same time/progressive aspect] about all the friends he <u>will no longer see</u> [after/simple aspect/sequence] every day.

2. When <u>the earthquake hit San Francisco</u> in 1989, Jeff <u>was</u> [at the same time] still at his office. He <u>had been trying</u> [started before and still in progress] to finish a project. He <u>had been working on</u> [started before and still in progress] it for over a week, and he <u>was</u> [at the same time] almost done. He <u>was just making</u> [at the same time] some final adjustments when the building <u>started</u> [at the same time] to move. When the quake <u>started</u> [at the same time], he quickly <u>got</u> [at the same time, or immediately after] under his desk. He <u>was</u> glad that he <u>had once read</u> [before] an article on what to do in earthquakes. He <u>had studied</u> [before] the article rather carefully, and as a result, he <u>knew</u> [at the same time] exactly what to do. As soon as things <u>started</u> [at the same time] falling off the shelves, Jeff <u>dove</u> [at the same time, or immediately after] for cover.

3. Denise <u>is</u> [general truth] quite a stylish dresser. She <u>thinks</u> [general truth] that it is important to be neat and well-groomed, and she always <u>wants</u> [recurrent action] to look her best. Every morning before she <u>leaves</u> [recurrent action] for work, <u>she looks at herself in the mirror</u>. She <u>checks</u> [at the same time] to make sure that she <u>has combed</u> [before] her hair and <u>hasn't put</u> [before] her make-up on too heavily. She <u>makes</u> [recurrent action] sure

5

             at the same time   general relationship   at the same time   recurrent action
that she is wearing colors that go nicely with the clothes she is wearing. She checks to see that her slip isn't
  at the same time   at the same time   recurrent action   before   general relationship
showing, and if her stockings are straight. She makes sure that the shoes she has chosen match the color of her
                    general truth   general truth
dress and her overcoat. She likes feeling confident and attractive, and feels that taking an extra minute in front
             general truth
of the mirror is worth the time.

Exercise 2

1. a, e   2. a, e   3. a, c, e   4. d   5. a, d   6. c, d   7. c, e, f   8. b   9. a, b   10. b, c   11. a, e

Exercise 3

1. am studying
2. was reading
3. get, are working
4. don't study, am not studying
5. speaks
6. was looking, discovered
7. reached, thought
8. am trying
9. was studying, heard
10. be sleeping

Exercise 4

1. c, d   2. a, c   3. a   4. a   5. d   6. d   7. a, c   8. b, c

Exercise 5

Alternative possible choices have been indicated.

1. had said (*said* is also possible, but with a change of meaning)   2. had conducted   3. has had   4. has visited   5. came, had been   6. have traveled   7. haven't slept/don't sleep   8. had completed, realized, weren't   9. have lived   10. has studied/studied

Exercise 6

1. a, b   2. b   3. b   4. a   5. a, b

Exercise 7

Alternative possible choices have been indicated.

1. has been raining/has rained
2. had worked/had been working
3. have found
4. has been finding/has found
5. has been cooking
6. had been looking/had looked, had left
7. have been trying/have tried
8. will have lived/will have been living
9. have been coming/have come; have moved/moved
10. have tried

Exercise 8

This can also be done orally by the whole class. Alternative possible choices have been indicated. It is necessary to do this exercise before Exercises 9 and 10.

(1) had/was having   (2) was working   (3) didn't get   (4) got   (5) had started   (6) heard   (7) pulled/was pulling   (8) walked   (9) shouted   (10) had just arrived   (11) kept dancing   (12) went   (13) were   (14) could tell   (15) had been dancing   (16) were sitting   (17) were   (18) chatted   (19) laughed   (20) was   (21) was   (22) went   (23) discovered   (24) had complained   (25) told   (26) obeyed   (27) got   (28) had   (29) was   (30) had complained/would complain   (31) thought/had thought   (32) had been invited/were invited   (33) were dancing

Exercise 9

You may wish to divide the class into groups or work in pairs with one student or group doing Exercise 9, and the other doing Exercise 10. The verb tenses in the three passages should be compared by the whole class. In most cases, the aspect choice remains the same in all three time frames. Here is one possible rewrite. Some additional adverbials have been added to make it more natural.

Every Friday night **has been** the same since I got my new room-mate, Louis the "dancing fool." My roommate **has** a dance party every Friday night. I **am working (work)** on Friday nights these days, so I **don't get** home until 10:00. By the time I **get** there, everyone **has started** dancing. I **hear** the music when I **pull** up in my car outside the apartment. When I **walk** into the room, everybody **shouts,** "Welcome Home!" because I **have just arrived,** but they always **keep** dancing, so I **go** into the kitchen to find something to drink. There **are** always several other people in the kitchen. I **can tell** that they **have been dancing** for some time, because they **are sitting** by an open window, and their clothes **are** damp with perspiration. We usually **chat** and **laugh** for a while. Just when I'm about ready to start dancing myself, there is a knock on the door. I **go** to answer it and **discover** a policeman standing in the hall. Apparently another neighbor **has complained** about the noise, and the policeman **tells** us to turn the music down. We always **obey,** of course. And although the party **gets** a little quieter, we still **have** just as much fun. I **am** usually somewhat surprised that anybody **has complained,** because I usually **think** all the other neighbors **have been invited** and **are dancing** with the rest of us.

Exercise 10

Here is one possible rewrite. Some additional adverbials have been added to make it more natural.

My roommate (we call him Louis, the dancing fool) **is going to have** a dance party next Friday night, and I think I know exactly what**'s going to happen. I'll be working** that night, so I **won't get** home until 10:00. By the time I **get** there, everyone **will have started** dancing. I **will hear** the music when I **pull** up in my car outside the apartment. When I **walk** into the room, everybody **will shout,** "Welcome Home!" because I **will have just arrived,** but they **will** just **keep** dancing, so I**'ll go** into the kitchen to find something to drink. There **will probably be** several other people in the kitchen. I **will be able to** tell that they **have been dancing** for some time, because they **will be sitting** by an open window, and their clothes **will be** damp with perspiration. We'll probably **chat** and **laugh** for a while. Just when I'm about ready to start dancing myself, there**'ll be** a knock on the door. I'll go to answer it and probably **discover** a policeman standing in the hall. Undoubtedly another neighbor **will have complained** about the noise, and the policeman **will tell** us to turn the music down. We **will obey,** of course. And although the party **will get** a little quieter, we'll probably still **have** just as much fun. **I'll be** a little surprised if anybody **complains,** because I **think** all the other neighbors **have been invited** and **will be dancing** with the rest of us.

Exercise 11

Answers will vary, but tense choice should be similar to the sample answers.

1. I had never eaten a hamburger; I thought everyone was rich.
2. when I am homesick; when I have done badly on a test.
3. snow, before I visited Colorado; couples kissing in public; before I came to the United States.
4. they will be very happy; they will be waving hello at the airport back home.
5. if I don't have time to exercise; if work is too crazy.
6. I thought babies came from a factory; I always pretended that I had my own horse.
7. since I was a student in high school; since I have been living in America.
8. I have been thinking about my family; I have been worrying about the TOEFL.
9. I will get married; I will find a good job; I will go back to my country.
10. I have never visited the Seychelles; I have never gotten 600 on the TOEFL.

Exercise 12

Answers will vary. Possible answers include:

1. Her boyfriend had gone to study in another country. She was missing him a lot.
   She had been thinking about her grandfather who had died.
2. He's meeting someone.
   His plane is late, and he's worrying about whether he will be able to catch his connecting flight.
3. She'll be graduating from college.
   She will have just gotten some good news about her scholarship.
4. They're looking for some buried treasure, but they haven't found it yet. They're planting trees according to the plan of a historic garden.
5. She had just won a contest.
   She had just gotten a letter from an old friend whom she thought was dead.
6. He's applying to schools.
   He hopes to get into a good university.
7. He doesn't have enough money to live comfortably.
   The city had to close the homeless shelter.
8. They had received a report of a fire.
   The alarm had sounded.

Exercise 13

An open-ended exercise. Possible interpretations include:

1. *I live by myself.* (I always do.)
   I'm living by myself. (This is a temporary situation.)
2. *I have lived by myself.* (This is something I have done in the past, and I may do it again, but right now I have a roommate.)
   I have been living by myself. (I am still living by myself.)
3. *He has paid the money.* (He doesn't owe us any more.)
   He has been paying the money. (But he still hasn't paid it all.)

4. *I studied when he left.* (I waited for him to leave before I started.)
   I was studying when he left. (I began to study before he left.)
   I had studied when he left. (I had finished studying before he left.)
5. *Robert Schilling worked in a factory.* (He doesn't work there now.)
   Robert Schilling has worked in a factory. (He still works there.)
6. *I studied for an hour.* (But now I have finished.)
   I have been studying for an hour. (And I'm not finished yet.)

Activities

Activity 1

This can be done orally or in writing. Aspect differences should remain the same.

Activity 2

This can be done orally or in writing.

Activity 3

Assign as a brief paragraph, and highlight any problems with tense sequence or aspect choice. Return to the students for correction/revision/questions. This can be used as a diagnostic to see whether additional work is needed with verb tenses (Units 18, 19, 20, and 30).

Activity 4

This can be done orally or in writing. Present perfect should be used to describe the living person, and simple past, past perfect, etc., should be used to describe the person who is deceased.

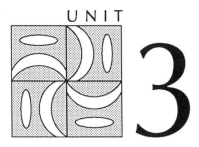

UNIT 3 Adverbials

Task

You may wish to bring newspapers into class and do this activity as an in-class review of *wh*-question formation.

Exercise 1

This can be done orally or with less-advanced classes as a written diagnostic of their control of *wh*-question formation. Answers will vary. Possible answers include:

1. When are we going to study adverbials?
   When should I answer this question?
2. Where do you want me to put this book?
   Where was the test yesterday?
3. How does our teacher speak?
   How do professional athletes run?
4. How frequently do you think about your family?
   Do you ever get homesick?
5. How do good students do their homework?
   How should people pick up broken glass from the floor?
6. When did you come to the United States?
   When did you graduate from high school?
7. How long have you been living here?
   How long have you been studying English?
8. How long are you planning to stay here?
   How long will you continue to study?
9. When do you eat lunch?
   What time does this class end?
10. Where are you from?
    From where did that plane depart?
11. Why are you reading that comic book?
    How come you're standing on your head?
12. Why do you worry about your English?
    Why can't Bambang begin his studies?
13. How can I get a good score on TOEFL?
    What's the best way to impress your teachers?

14. Why are you reading that book?
    Why do you listen to English-language TV?
15. Why are you studying English?
    What are you hoping for in your future?
16. When will you get married?
    When will you start working?
17. Why is John working nights?
    Why is he worried all the time?
18. How long will Jose study in an intensive English program?
    How long will his uncle nag him about studying?
19. How long can you stay here on a student visa?
    How long will your parents continue to support you?
20. Why does John need money?
    Why is he going to the bookstore?

Exercise 2

This exercise and Exercise 3 have a dual purpose: to familiarize students with the **meaning and use** of adverbials, and just as important, to give them practice **identifying phrases and clauses,** the basic forms that are the building blocks of complex written English.

1. HOW; manner; adverb
2. WHERE; place/position; adverbial phrase
3. WHEN; time; adverbial clause
4. WHERE; place/direction; adverbial phrase
5. HOW; manner; adverbial clause
6. WHERE; place/position; adverbial phrase
7. WHEN; time/when; adverbial clause
8. WHY; purpose; adverbial phrase
9. HOW MANY; degree; adverbial clause
10. HOW; manner/means; adverbial phrase
11. HOW LONG; time/duration; adverbial phrase
12. WHEN; time/when; adverbial clause
13. HOW SAFE; degree; adverbial phrase
14. WHY; purpose; adverbial phrase
15. HOW PUZZLED; degree; adverb
16. WHY; reason; adverbial clause
17. HOW AGGRESSIVE; degree; adverb
18. WHY; cause and effect; adverbial clause
19. HOW OFTEN; frequency; adverb
20. WHY; purpose; adverbial phrase

Exercise 3

Meaning		Form		
		Adverbs	Adverbial Phrases	Adverbial Clauses
WHERE	PLACE		6, 17, 21	
WHEN	TIME — WHEN		1, 3, 4, 9, 11, 22	14
HOW LONG	TIME — DURATION		7, 8, 15	
HOW OFTEN	FREQUENCY			16
HOW	MANNER	10, 12	2	
HOW MUCH	DEGREE			19, 20
WHY	PURPOSE AND REASON		5, 13, 18	
	CAUSE AND EFFECT			

Exercise 4

This is an open-ended exercise.

How Often (Frequency)	VERB PHRASE	How (Manner)	Where (Place)	When (Time)	Why (Cause and Effect)
1. always	are trying to change the way they look				because neither one is very pleased with his appearance
2.	go about it	differently			
3.	tries to increase the size of his muscles	by lifting weights	at a gym near his house		
4. usually	goes		there	at the same time; every day	

How Often (Frequency)	VERB PHRASE	How (Manner)	Where (Place)	When (Time)	Why (Cause and Effect)
5.	drinks special vitamin supplements				to gain weight
6. twice a day	works out	vigorously		in the morning and in the afternoon	
7. usually	starts out		on an exercise bike		to warm up his muscles
8.	exercises his upper body			on Mondays, Wednesdays, and Fridays	
9.	does exercises			On Tuesdays, Thursdays, and Saturdays	to develop the muscles of his lower body
10. never	works out			on Sundays	so his muscles can have a chance to rest
11. always	seems to be trying to lose weight	by going on special weight-reducing diets		whenever he feels too heavy	
12. usually	drinks a special diet drink			at breakfast and lunch	
13. sometimes	doesn't eat anything			after breakfast	in order to save a few calories
14.	tries not to snack			between meals	
15. usually	is really hungry			when he gets home	
16. often	goes	directly	to the kitchen		to find something to eat
17. never	lost more than a few pounds			permanently	
18. always	is looking for a magic way to lose weight	without having to diet or exercise			

Are there any sentences in which the adverbials don't follow the basic order listed above? Which sentences? What was the order?

#6 — Adverbial of frequency came after the verb phrase.

#9 — Adverbial of time came at the beginning of the sentence.

#15 — Adverb of frequency came between verb (BE) and complement.

#17 — Adverb of manner came before verb phrase.

#18 — Adverb of frequency came between the auxiliary and the main verb.

Exercise 5

Answers may vary. These are all possible. In some cases, there is only one correct order.

1. Every few months Gladstone Gulp goes on a new diet because he feels heavy;
   Gladstone Gulp goes on a new diet every few months, because he feels heavy.
2. He regularly uses diet pills to increase his metabolism;
   He uses diet pills regularly to increase his metabolism;
   To increase his metabolism, he uses diet pills regularly.
3. He infrequently rides an exercise bicycle very hard to use up calories;
   To use up calories, he infrequently rides an exercise bicycle very hard.
4. He sometimes trades diet plans with his friend Biff;
   Sometimes he trades diet plans with his friend Biff.
5. He reads carefully about every new diet in magazines whenever he can;
   Whenever he can, he carefully reads in magazines about every new diet;
   In magazines, he carefully reads about every new diet whenever he can.
6. He doesn't always follow their directions carefully.
7. He usually drinks a special vitamin supplement to make sure he gets proper nutrition;
   To make sure he gets proper nutrition, he usually drinks a special vitamin supplement.

Exercise 6

Answers will vary. Possible answers include:

1. She goes to school every day; He thinks about his family every day.
2. Good students always do their homework carefully; To assemble a bomb, one must set the fuse carefully to avoid a premature explosion.
3. He speaks English very well; She cooks Indonesian food very well.
4. Joe always brushes his teeth before bedtime; Mary says her prayers before bedtime.
5. John plays tennis outdoors; Mary sometimes takes a nap outdoors.
6. Ivan watches TV occasionally; Kathy occasionally forgets to do her homework.
7. Maria sings better than anyone else in her family; Marvin speaks Japanese better than anyone else in his family.
8. Steve automatically locks his car whenever he parks it; Denise automatically hangs up her coat as soon as she comes home from work.
9. Janet makes friends with considerable difficulty; Peter speaks Chinese with considerable difficulty.
10. Jacob usually does his homework after class; Naomi likes to ask her teacher questions after class.

Exercise 7

This is an open-ended exercise. There are a number of possible reasons for the order. For less-advanced classes, the exercise can be used for additional practice in identifying the form and meaning of adverbials.

1. (a) place, adverbial phrase; (b) place, adverbial phrase; (c) time, adverb
   Reasons: (a) comes before; (b) because it is more specific; Indefinite time adverbs can come before the main verb.
2. (a) frequency, adverb; (b) reason, adverbial phrase
   Reasons: Frequency adverbs come before the verb, reason adverbials come after the verb.
3. (a) time, adverbial phrase; (b) time, adverbial phrase; (c) frequency, adverb; (d) purpose, adverbial phrase
   Reasons: Three adverbials have variable order, and precede adverbial of reason.
4. (a) frequency, adverb; (b) manner, adverb; (c) time, adverbial phrase
   Reasons: These follow basic order of frequency–manner–time.
5. (a) frequency, adverb; (b) time, adverbial phrase; (c) reason: adverbial phrase
   Reasons: These follow basic order of frequency–time–reason.
6. (a) frequency, adverb; (b) frequency, adverbial phrase; (c) reason; adverbial phrase
   Reasons: Single-word adverbs of frequency usually come before the verb phrase, frequency adverbial phrases usually come after the verb phrase; adverbials of reason usually come at the end.
7. (a) frequency, adverb; (b) manner, adverbial phrase
   Reasons: Shorter adverbs usually come before longer ones; frequency adverbs come before adverbs of manner.
8. (a) frequency, adverb; (b) manner, adverbial phrase; (c) purpose, adverbial phrase
   Reasons: These follow basic order.
9. (a) frequency, adverb; (b) manner; adverbial phrase
   Reasons: These follow basic order.
10. (a) frequency, adverbial phrase; (b) reason, adverbial phrase
    Reasons: Adverbial phrases of frequency come after the verb BE but before reason adverbs.
11. (a) frequency, adverb; (b) reason, adverbial phrase
    Reasons: Adverbs of frequency come after the verb BE and before the complement.
12. (a) frequency, adverb; (b) place; adverbial phrase; (c) place; adverbial phrase; (d) reason; adverbial phrase
    Reasons: Frequency adverb comes before the verb; the more specific place adverbial comes before the more general one; reason comes at the end.
13. (a) sentence adverbial; (b) manner, adverb; (c) place, adverbial phrase; (d) time, adverbial phrase
    Reasons: Sentence adverbials usually come at the beginning of the sentence (see Focus 5 and Unit 13); other adverbials follow basic order of manner–place–time.

Exercise 8

This is an open-ended exercise. It may not be appropriate for less-advanced classes. There may be several possible explanations. Possible explanations include:

1. BEFORE: Order expresses the logical relationship of cause and effect.
2. AFTER: Order emphasizes the contrast introduced by "on the other hand."
3. AFTER: Basic order — no special emphasis.
4. BEFORE: Emphasizes cause; underscores logical relation of cause and effect.

5. BEFORE: Follows the chronological order of events.
6. BEFORE: Emphasizes the "although" clause, to make the logical connection between the two clauses more obvious.
7. AFTER: Follows the chronological order of events.
8. AFTER: Order expresses the logical relationship between cause and effect.
9. BEFORE: Follows the chronological order of events.

Activities

Activity 1

Can be done orally, or in written form as additional practice/diagnosis of *wh*-question formation.

Activity 2

Can be done orally in pairs or small groups, or individually in written form. Can be used to diagnose understanding of active/passive and article use. Here are some possible paraphrases:

- The stock market has crashed.
- The United States population is moving West.
- The new budget was termed a disaster.
- The President is visiting Asia.
- The United States will protest the use of gill nets.
- The Pope will visit China.
- The drought is expected to worsen.
- There is a new plan to improve transit services.
- Test scores are improving in the public schools.
- A link has been found between diet and heart disease.
- Cancer is reported to be increasing.
- There has been a major growth in the number of foreign students in the United States.
- There has been a big shake-up at the Kremlin.

Activity 3

Students should be reminded to pay attention to adverbial order as they do this activity.

Activity 4

This activity practices adverbials of purpose and reason, and can be used to diagnose the need for additional practice (Unit 16). The final presentation can be either oral or written.

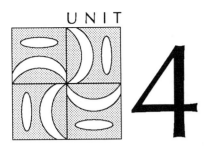

UNIT 4 — Passive Verbs

Task

Most students enjoy this topic a great deal. You can use the Task as a diagnostic activity by asking the students to write their opinions, as such a topic naturally elicits use of passive forms.

Exercise 1

1. is being made
2. had been left
3. was built
4. is produced
5. can be read
6. will be sent
7. was being planned
8. might have been needed

Exercise 2

1. is constructing
2. had forgotten
3. established
4. manufactures
5. can obtain
6. will require
7. were duplicating
8. might have discovered

Exercise 3

Answers will vary. Possible answers for **Exercise 1** sentences include:

1. Progress is being made in the negotiation about the free trade agreement.
   We'll visit a factory where wine is being made.
2. Some cake had been left behind after the party, so I ate it.
   Nothing had been left for the others.
3. The Taj Mahal was built in the seventeenth century.
   In desert places a hundred years ago, most of the housing was built of mud.
4. Gunpowder is produced by mixing saltpeter and sulfur.
   Electricity is produced by hydroelectric generators.
5. This can be read in just a few minutes.
   Some writing can be read by machines.
6. Your TOEFL results will be sent in a few weeks.
   The winner of the contest will be sent to Hawaii for a free vacation.
7. A decrease in standard of living was being noticed by most people as they thought about voting for a new government.
   The young girl in the funny hat hoped that she was being noticed.

8. She brought lots of food to the party because she thought it might have been needed.

I'm glad you brought money with you. It might have been needed to pay the bill.

Possible answers for **Exercise 2** sentences include:

1. A new factory is being constructed.

   The house next door is being constructed entirely of steel and glass.
2. When we got to the hotel, we realized that one of our suitcases had been forgotten at the airport.

   By this century, the original purpose of Stonehenge had been forgotten.
3. The first British colony in North America was established in 1608.

   General Motors was established by Henry Ford.
4. Silk is manufactured in China.

   A lot of equipment is manufactured by machine.
5. A driver's license can be obtained at the Department of Motor Vehicles.

   Cigarettes can be obtained almost anywhere.
6. You will be required to come at 8:00.

   A high score on TOEFL will be required for admission to graduate programs.
7. The midterm examinations were being duplicated, so I couldn't wait in the office.

   We asked one worker to do something else because her efforts were being duplicated by someone else.
8. North America might have been discovered by Viking explorers before Columbus arrived.

   I'm not completely sure, but I think a new vaccine for hepatitis might have been discovered recently.

Exercise 4

1. Urdu, Punjabi, Sindhi, Baluchi, Pashtu, and English *are spoken* in Pakistan.
2. Lapis lazuli *has been* mined for centuries in Afghanistan.
3. Snails *are considered* a great delicacy in France.
4. Rice *is eaten* by people throughout Asia.
5. More beer *is consumed* per capita in Australia than in any other country.
6. Cats *were worshiped* in Ancient Egypt.
7. A new system of high-resolution television *has been developed* in Japan.
8. The games of baseball and basketball *were invented* in America.

Exercise 5

Answers will vary. Possible answers will include:

Batik is made in Indonesia. The best batik is produced by hand. The cloth is painted with wax and then it is dyed. The cloth is used for clothing and decoration. It is exported to many other countries.

Exercise 6

This is an open-ended exercise.

1. *agent:* grandfather; *recipient:* this painting; *subject:* this painting; no grammatical object
2. *agent:* Romans; *recipient:* an elaborate system of aqueducts; *subject:* Romans; *object:* an elaborate system of aqueducts

3. *agent:* our teacher; *recipient:* we; *subject:* we; no grammatical object
4. *agent:* all students; *recipient:* grammar; *subject:* all students; *object:* grammar
5. *agent:* many government officials; *recipient:* French; *subject:* French; no grammatical object
6. *agent:* Denise; *recipient:* Peter's easygoing attitude; *subject:* Denise; *object:* Peter's easygoing attitude

Exercise 7

This is an open-ended exercise.

(1) The Nazca Lines <u>were not discovered</u> [R] until the 1930s, when they <u>were first noticed</u> [R] by airplane pilots [A] flying over Peru's Atacama Desert. (2) They consist of huge pictures, several kilometers in size, that <u>were drawn</u> [R] in the desert. (3) They depict such things such as birds, spiders, and abstract geometrical designs. (4) These pictures <u>were made</u> [R] more than 3,000 years ago by removing stones and dirt over large areas to expose the different-colored soil beneath.

(5) The amazing thing about the Nazca Lines is that none of these pictures <u>can be seen</u> [R] by people on the ground [A]. (6) They are so huge that they <u>can only be seen</u> [R] from a great height. (7) The pictures <u>were constructed</u> [R] with incredible precision. (8) Exactly how such precise measurements <u>were made</u> [R] still <u>hasn't been satisfactorily explained</u> [R]. (9) It seems impossible that the primitive construction techniques that existed 3,000 years ago <u>could have been used</u> to create such gigantic, perfectly constructed designs.

(10) Who made these gigantic pictures and why? (11) <u>Were</u> they <u>intended to be used</u> [R] as offerings for the gods, as some people have suggested? (12) Or, as others believe, <u>were</u> they <u>created</u> [R] as "direction signs" for visitors from other planets [R]? (13) No one knows. (14) One thing <u>is known</u> [R]: The reasons for and methods of construction <u>have been obliterated</u> [R] with time, but the pictures <u>have been preserved</u> for at least 2,000 — and maybe even 3,000 — years!

Exercise 8

1. were
2. got/was; be
3. being
4. got/was
5. get
6. got/was
7. get
8. get/be

Exercise 9

This is an open-ended exercise. These are the most probable explanations for using passive, but others may also be possible.

1. generic announcement
2. to connect ideas in different clauses (*Mary* is the subject of both clauses.)
3. agent is obvious from context
4. agent is obvious from context
5. agent is unknown/to connect ideas in different clauses more clearly
6. to emphasize recipient
7. to emphasize recipient
8. agent is unknown
9. agent is obvious from context
10. agent is obvious from context/to connect ideas in different clauses more clearly

Exercise 10

This is an open-ended exercise. Explanations like those above will apply to the passives as appropriate.

(1) are often discriminated against   (2) may be discriminated against   (3) may not be allowed   (4) are not allowed   (5) are not allowed   (6) is being eliminated
(7) has made   (8) have not come   (9) were not allowed   (10) were forced   (11) were changed, is no longer permitted   (12) were also forced
(13) are still being fought   (14) are still paid   (15) are still confronted   (16) are not allowed, can be fired   (17) to be improving, has been made

Exercise 11

1. The Nazca Lines were constructed approximately 2,000 years ago.
2. The lesson was assigned for next week.
3. This picture was painted when Picasso was 12 years old.
4. My briefcase got taken, but it was found and turned in to the Lost and Found Office **by someone in my English class.** (*Second agent cannot be deleted — there is important information that the person was someone in my English class.*)
5. Many foreign students don't need scholarships because they are being supported **by friends or relatives.** (*Agent cannot be deleted.*)
6. I would never guess that these poems were translated **by children.** (*Agent cannot be deleted.*)

Exercise 12

(1) was released/has been released; took place   (2) was disproved/has been disproved   (3) widened   (4) increased; decreased; are made/were made   (6) dropped; earned   (7) rose; declined

Exercise 13

(1) began   (2) were intended; were called   (3) started/was started; was referred to   (4) measured   (5) comprise   (6) stand; know; were written; existed

Exercise 14

(1) was built   (2) was designed; serve   (3) consider   (4) is made   (5) intended; be located   (6) copy   (7) planned; consist; was used   (8) was imprisoned; died; got; implement   (9) was realized

Exercise 15

(1) being developed/developing; revolutionize   (2) emerging   (3) be immunized/immunize   (4) work   (5) be split; be attached   (6) are injected; reproduce; occur; be exposed   (7) appear; produce   (8) attack; seem   (9) enable; be used

Activities

Activity 1

This is a good diagnostic or testing activity.

Activity 2

A hot topic. Care may be needed in some classes to ensure that the discussion doesn't become too volatile.

Activities 3 and 4

These can be used to test student mastery of forms and use of passive voice.

Activity 5

A logical carryover from the Task, to be used if your class is particularly intrigued by the preliminary discussions.

UNIT 5

One-Word and Phrasal Modals

Additional Grammar Notes:
Question and Negative Forms of Phrasal Modals

THE QUESTION AND NEGATIVE FORMS OF PHRASAL MODALS ARE LIKE OTHER AUXILIARIES IN ENGLISH:	
• **phrasal modals with BE** (be able to/going to/about to/supposed to/allowed to)	• **phrasal modals without BE** (have to, used to)
• affirmative statements: (a) Victor **is/was able to** speak Spanish.	(b) Victor **has/had to** speak English in class.
• negative statements: (c) He **is/wasn't supposed to** speak Spanish at school.	(d) He **does/didn't have to** speak it at home.
• question/short answer: (e) **Is/was** he **allowed to** speak it at home? Yes, he probably **is/was**.	(f) **Does/did** he **have to** do study English every day? No, he **does/didn't**.

YOU CAN COMBINE ONE-WORD AND PHRASAL MODALS TO MAKE STATEMENTS CONCERNING:	
• advisability: (g) A fireman **should be able to** carry at least 150 pounds. (h) Poor people **shouldn't have to** pay the same taxes as rich people. • necessity: (i) I **must be allowed to** speak with the doctor. (j) Children **mustn't be able** to open medicine bottles.	• future predictions: (k) I **may be able to** get some extra tickets. (l) We **shouldn't have to** wait too long. (m) You **might not be allowed to** bring a guest.

22

> YOU CAN COMBINE CERTAIN PHRASAL MODALS WITH EACH OTHER
> TO MAKE STATEMENTS CONCERNING:

- **necessity:**
    - (n) A fireman **has to be able to** carry at least 250 pounds.
    - (o) In order for plants to be healthy, they **have got to be able to** get plenty of sunshine.
    - (p) Children **have to be allowed to** choose their own friends.
- **advisability:**
    - (q) You **ought to be able to** speak French if you want a job in Paris.
    - (r) Dogs **aren't supposed to be allowed to ride** on buses.
- **future predictions:**
    - (s) I'm not **going to be able to** come to your party.
    - (t) I'm not **going to be allowed to** bring a guest.
    - (u) I'm **going to have to** leave.

Task

This can be used as a diagnostic for both modals and causative verbs, either by using the two sets of sentences (reasons and difficulties) or by checking the paragraph on advantages and disadvantages for correct form and use. Alternatively, the lists can be generated in pairs or small groups and presented to the rest of the class.

Exercise 1

Modal meaning varies according to context. Possible alternative interpretations are also given. In all cases, the first interpretation is the most likely.

1. permission
2. ability/request
3. request
4. future activity
5. ability
6. advisability/obligation
7. permission
8. necessity/request
9. advisability/obligation
10. inference
11. future possibility/inference
12. permission
13. inference
14. future possibility/inference
15. request

Exercise 2

Answers will vary. Possible answers include:

1. I must make my bed.   I must go to work.
2. You should write letters every month.   You can call them on the phone if you have enough money.
3. You should study harder.   You should make friends with a really smart classmate.
4. I can play the piano.   I can cook delicious bean soup.
5. I might take a vacation next summer.   I could pass the TOEFL next semester.
6. You can't drink beer in class.   You can't hit your teacher.
7. I can't water-ski.   I can't speak Lithuanian.

Exercise 3

Answers will vary. Possible answers include:

1. I have to make my bed.   I have to go to work.
2. You ought to write letters every month.   You ought to call them on the phone if you have enough money.
3. You had better study harder.   You had better make friends with a really smart classmate.
4. I am able to play the piano.   I'm able to cook delicious bean soup.
5. (No phrasal modals can be used to express this meaning.) I might take a vacation next summer.   I could pass the TOEFL next semester.
6. You aren't allowed to drink beer in class.   You'd better not hit your teacher.
7. I'm not able to water-ski.   I'm not able to speak Lithuanian.

Exercise 4

This is an open-ended exercise.

(1) *have to go* — **necessity**   (2) *can't eat* — **ability**   (3) *[a]m supposed to be* — **obligation**; *mustn't be* — **obligation**; *[wi]ll cancel* — **future activity**   (4) *had better leave* — **advisability**   (5) *is supposed to come* — **obligation**   (6) *ought to go* — **advisability**   (7) *[i]s going to tell* — **future activity**; *have to take* — **necessity**   (8) *[a]m supposed to brush* — **advisability**; *can't find* — **ability**   (9) *won't be able to eat* — **future ability**; *[a]m not supposed to eat* — **advisability**   (10) *[a]m going to be* — **future activity**

Exercise 5

1. future activity, necessity
2. future activity, ability
3. future activity, permission
4. necessity, ability
5. necessity, permission
6. advisability, ability
7. permission
8. necessity, ability

Exercise 6

Alternative possible choices have been indicated.

1. must be allowed to
2. should(n't) be allowed to
3. should have to
4. (has to/has got to) be able to
5. am not going to be able to
6. have to be able to
7. (had better/ought to) be able to

Exercise 7

Answers will vary. Sample dialogues might be:

1. Do you have to take the bus to get to school?

    No, I don't. I get a ride with a friend.

    What time do you have to leave home?

    About 15 minutes before class.

    My partner doesn't have to leave her house until just before class, because she gets a ride in a friend's car.

2. Are we allowed to smoke here?

   No, we aren't. We can't smoke in the classrooms at all.

   Where can we smoke?

   There's a lounge on the first floor. I think we can smoke there.

   We aren't allowed to smoke in class, but my partner thinks that we can smoke in the lounge downstairs.

3. Are you supposed to do any chores at your apartment?

   I'm supposed to take out the garbage.

   How often are you supposed to do that?

   I'm supposed to do it every day, but sometimes I forget.

   My partner is supposed to take out the garbage every day, but sometimes he forgets to do it.

4. Were you able to do the homework last night?

   No, I wasn't. I was too busy.

   Why weren't you able to do it?

   My uncle was visiting from Korea, and we went to a restaurant.

   My partner wasn't able to do her homework last night, because she had a visit from her uncle.

5. Are you going to go anywhere on vacation?

   Yes, I'm going to visit Yosemite.

   How are you going get there?

   I'm going to go with a friend who has a car.

   My partner's going to drive to Yosemite with a friend during the vacation.

Exercise 8

Answers will vary. Possible answers include:

- People shouldn't have to go to work wherever the government sends them.
- People shouldn't have to work without pay on community projects.
- People shouldn't have to follow one particular religion.
- People should have to send their children to school.
- People shouldn't have to always obey their leaders.
- People should have to vote in elections.
- People should have to report criminals to the police.
- People shouldn't have to get permission to leave the country.
- People shouldn't have to serve in the army.
- People should have to pay taxes.

Exercise 9

Answers will vary. Possible answers include:

- Fluent speakers should be able to read a newspaper.
- Fluent speakers don't have to be able to understand native speakers perfectly when they are speaking to each other.

- Fluent speakers must be able to understand native speakers when they are speaking to foreigners.
- Fluent speakers should be able to speak correctly enough that people can understand what they mean.
- Fluent speakers don't have to have a perfect accent.
- Fluent speakers should never be afraid to make mistakes.
- Fluent speakers don't have to be able to discuss abstract philosophy.
- Fluent speakers must be able to take care of day-to-day needs.
- Fluent speakers don't have to sound exactly like native speakers.
- Fluent speakers should be able to read and understand literature and poetry.

Activities

Activity 1

The priorities and reasons can be written as a diagnostic or testing activity to check understanding and use of modal forms.

Activity 2

This exercise can be used at the beginning of the course along with the other self-assessment activities such as Unit 1, Activity 5, and Unit 4, Activity 1, and the Task in Unit 16. The self-assessment can be written as a paragraph, "I think my FSI rating should be _____ because of the following reasons..." to test students' mastery of modal forms, in addition to providing them with an opportunity to assess their productive and receptive language skills.

Activity 3

This can be done in pairs, small groups, or individually. Students may need help "decoding" want ad abbreviations.

Activity 4

This activity can be used as a testing activity by asking students to write paragraphs rather than want ads.

Activity 5

You may want to expand this activity for certain classes (immigrants, new Americans), to give them additional information of life-skills, job hunting, etc. In such a case, it would be a good idea for you to bring in want ads for the whole class, and have them do the activity in pairs or small groups.

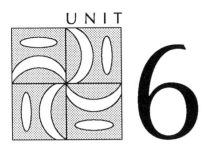

UNIT 6

Infinitives

Task

This can be used as a diagnostic by asking students to write full-sentence answers to the discussion questions. Such possible answers will include:

What things does he still need to do?
   He still needs to buy a present for Mary.
   He still needs to say good-bye to Prof. Montaigne.

What things does he need Mary to do?
   He needs Mary to drive him to the airport.
   He needs Mary to understand why he's going to France.

What things does he want Charley to do?
   He wants Charley to help move boxes to Mary's garage.
   He wants Charley to clean the kitchen.

What things does he want Charley not to do?
   He doesn't want Charley to tell Mary about giving John the address of his old girlfriend.
   He doesn't want Charley to forget about helping to move boxes.

Exercise 1

This is an open-ended exercise.

(1) *to collect stamps* — object of verb *likes*   (2) *getting them* — object of verb *likes*; *collecting stamps* — object of preposition   (3) *to get at least one stamp* — object of verb *tried*   (4) *to do* — adjective complement   (5) *writing to the post offices* — object of verb *tried*   (6) *looking in commercial stamp catalogs* — object of verb *suggested*; *finding rare or unusual stamps* — noun complement   (7) *corresponding with stamp collectors* — object of verb *begun*; *to send him stamps* — object of verb *asked*   (8) *to do it* — adjective complement; *to do the same thing* — object of verb *urged*   (9) *learning about other countries* — object of verb *enjoys*; *collecting stamps* — subject of verb *is*

Exercise 2

1. Morris claims that he was born in Russia.
2. We expected that you had already done the assignment.
3. The teacher said, "Do not forget to do your homework."
4. We expected that John would be studying when we got home.
5. If my sister is left alone on a Saturday night, she is never happy.

Exercise 3

Answers will vary. Possible answers include:

1. They expect me to study hard. They expect me to do my best. They expect me not to waste my time. They expect me not to forget to write them often.
2. I like to treat them politely. I like to treat them in a friendly way. I like to be treated with respect. I like to be treated in a friendly way.
3. She expects me to open my book. She expects me to stop talking with my friends. She expects me to have done my homework before class. She expects me to have studied the assignment.
4. I plan to take a vacation. I plan to go home for a visit. I plan to be taking the TOEFL. I plan to be saying good-bye to my friends and teachers.

Exercise 4

1. Malcolm is speaking.
2. People turn in their room keys.
3. Peter will bring her book.
4. My sister will stay after the party.
5. Gladstone will lose 30 pounds by Christmas.
6. The friend put a frog in the teacher's desk.
7. Norman didn't stay up late.
8. The children started working.

Exercise 5

agreed	demanded	tended
appear	pretended	learned
claimed	hesitated	neglected
care	offered	hopes
deserved	refused	waiting
decided	seem	

Exercise 6

Answers will vary. Possible answers include:

1. to be something he or she is not; to be able to do something he or she can't really do.
2. to give his child a good education; to make sure his children are healthy.
3. to read and write; to follow instructions.
4. to take foreign vacations; to buy whatever they want.
5. to be getting worse and worse; to be improving.
6. to raise their hands in class; to answer questions voluntarily.
7. to help other people; to share their money or possessions with others.
8. to help a friend in trouble; to spend time with his or her friends.
9. to be punished for their crimes; to get a fair trial.
10. to become wealthy and famous; to live in a happy family.
11. to think for themselves; to ask questions about things they don't understand.
12. to become adults; to be old enough to drive a car.
13. to like and respect their students; to know answers to their students' questions.
14. to tell a lie; to commit a crime.
15. to perform difficult actions effortlessly; to be competing against themselves.

Exercise 7

Answers will vary. Possible answers include:

1. My partner often neglects to do her homework.
   My partner often neglects to write her mother.
2. My partner learned to take lecture notes in English class.
   She learned to ask questions when she doesn't understand.
3. My partner can't afford to go out to dinner every night.
   She can't afford to phone her parents very often.
4. My partner would never hesitate to accept help from a friend.
   She would never hesitate to accept money from her rich uncle.
5. My partner would refuse to cheat on a TOEFL test.
   My partner would refuse to steal money from a friend.
6. My partner thinks he deserves to pass the TOEFL.
   He thinks he deserves to get an A in this class.
7. My partner tends to be shy in a room full of strangers.
   My partner tends to be very outgoing in a room full of strangers.
8. My partner pretended to be a cowboy.
   He pretended to be invisible.
9. They appeared to be nervous.
   They appeared to be curious and friendly.
10. My partner would never care to meet Madonna.
    He would never care to meet Cardinal Ratzinger.

Exercise 8

Answers will vary. Possible answers include:

1. My friend reminded me to pay him the money I owed him.
   I want to remind you to pay the rent before the first of the month.
2. The doctor warned me not to forget to take my medicine.
   My wife warned me not to forget to stop at the store after work.
3. John convinced Charley to help him move his boxes.
   It's easy to convince most people to help others.
4. Let's hire someone to work in the garden.
   We hired a secretary to work on that big project.
5. The government requires people to pay fines if they break traffic laws.
   All movie theaters require people to pay in order to see the film.
6. My parents forbid me to marry someone with a different religion.
   Fifty years ago many states in the southern United States forbade blacks to marry whites.
7. Let's invite Nancy to join us in the hot tub.
   The Boy Scouts won't invite gay people to join their organization.
8. Our teacher taught us to speak clearly.
   Mary teaches children to speak French.

9. Most countries allow their citizens to leave the country without special permission.

   They wouldn't allow the students to leave the room until the test was finished.

10. The government orders all parents to send their children to school.

    The boss has ordered me to send this by Express Mail.

11. The president urged everyone to vote for him.

    I'm urging you to vote for someone else.

12. My parents trust me to spend my money wisely.

    That child trusts his friend not to tell anyone their secret.

13. My mother told me to eat more vegetables.

    The doctor told me to eat fewer fatty foods.

14. Good teachers encourage their students to ask questions.

    I encourage you to ask the boss for a raise.

15. The bad weather forced us to leave the picnic early.

    I don't want to force you to leave before you're ready.

Exercise 9

Answers will vary. Possible answers include:

1. My partner likes to do the dishes, but he prefers someone else to do the cooking.

   My partner likes to cook, but he likes someone else to do the dishes.

2. My partner expects to study hard, and he expects his teacher to answer his questions.

   My partner expects to work in the same kind of business as his uncle after he finishes school, and he expects his uncle to help him get a job.

3. My partner has asked to leave the room, and he has asked me to go with him.

   My partner has asked to be excused from the homework, and he has asked the teacher to give him the excuse.

4. My partner needs to get a haircut, but he needs someone else to cut his hair.

   My partner needs to write a statement of purpose for her university application, but she needs a native English speaker to check over her grammar.

5. My partner has arranged to leave on vacation right after school, and she has arranged for me to pick up her grade report.

   My partner has arranged to meet his friend after school, and has arranged for his friend to join him at his uncle's house.

Exercise 10

1. Mary has requested John to write a long letter once a week.
2. Mary would prefer (for) John to postpone his trip until next year.
3. She has decided to try to visit him while he's there.
4. He didn't expect her to be upset by the news of his plans.
5. Mary's father arranged for John to get a very cheap ticket.
6. John neglected to apply for a passport.
7. French law requires John to report to the police when he arrives.
8. John has encouraged Mary to begin to study French herself.
9. John never intended for Mary to feel hurt that he is leaving.

Exercise 11

1. John was warned not to fall in love with a French girl.
2. John was asked to study in a special accelerated program.
3. John was encouraged to apply for a scholarship.
4. John was chosen to receive a partial tuition discount.
5. Mary was convinced to give John permission to leave for a year.
6. John was taught to use French for all daily activities.
7. John was invited to have his meals with a French family.
8. French cooking is considered to be the best in Europe.

Exercise 12

Answers will vary. Possible answers include:

1. to look out for their own best interests; to do the right thing.
2. to ask questions about everything; to try different kinds of food.
3. to help their students; to lighten up and stop being workaholics.
4. to quiet down; to be more considerate of others.
5. to say no to drugs; to say no to sex; to say no to their parents.
6. to ask questions when they don't understand; to thank their teachers at the end of the semester.
7. to make themselves at home; to help themselves, and be relaxed.
8. to pay the same percentage of taxes as middle-class people; to contribute to charities.

Exercise 13

Answers will vary. Possible answers include:

1. to look both ways before you cross the street; to send your teacher a card for Christmas.
2. to sleep late on Saturday mornings; to have long conversations with friends.
3. to get drunk before taking the TOEFL; to smoke marijuana in front of a policeman.
4. to have a child become a doctor; to hold a grandchild in their arms.
5. to give good grades to lazy students; to give up her weekends to tutor lazy students.
6. to understand native speakers; to concentrate on homework when the sun is shining.
7. to work hard if you want to succeed; to do your homework before you come to class.
8. to learn a foreign language; to adjust to living in a new culture.

Activities

Activities 1 and 2

These can be used as testing activities.

Activity 3

This will provide opportunities for natural use of common verb + infinitive patterns. This activity adapts well to whole-class discussion.

Activity 4

This activity provides more explicit discussion of good strategies for independent language learning. It is appropriate to follow it up with a brief whole-class discussion of the issues.

Activity 5

The presentation can be written or oral.

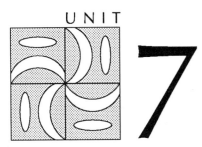

UNIT 7 Gerunds

Task

This can be used as a diagnostic activity by having students write their list of the activities they enjoy doing, enjoy not doing, and don't enjoy doing as full sentences.

Exercise 1

1. When we are asked for money all the time, we hate it.
2. I really appreciate that you have taken such good care of my dog while I was on vacation.
3. They suspected that he took/had taken the money.
4. We didn't plan for the fact that they would/might have problems with the homework.
5. I think John resents the fact that he wasn't invited to the party.

Exercise 2

Answers will vary. Possible answers include:

1. I enjoy sleeping late.   I enjoy eating a fancy breakfast.
   I enjoy not getting up early.   I enjoy not going to bed until late.

2. I hate doing grammar homework.   I hate writing compositions.
   I don't mind other people helping me with my homework.   I don't mind other people asking questions in class.

3. I like giving help and advice to my friends.   I like giving people silly presents.
   I like people giving me massages.   I like other people giving me advice on my problems.

4. Being in a university requires reading a lot of books.   Being in the university requires studying several hours every night.
   Being in a university typically requires having passed the TOEFL.   Being in a university typically requires having filled out an application.

Exercise 3

1. Jeff lives in San Francisco.
2. You're helping us get ready for the party.
3. Peter will be looking for a new job.
4. Matt won't leave San Francisco.
5. John is spending a year overseas.

33

6. She (another woman — not Miss Manners) behaved rudely.
7. We were going to leave for the trip, but we couldn't change our tickets.
8. You were supposed to do the singing and dancing in the school talent show.

Exercise 4

recommend   avoid
suggest   quit
deny   practice
consider   include
admit   resist
can't help   keep on
give up   keep

Exercise 5

Answers will vary. Possible answers include:

Most doctors recommend losing weight.   Most doctors recommend giving up smoking.

They suggest following a system of diet and exercise.   They suggest reducing cholesterol intake whenever possible.

I don't deny needing to lose weight, so I considered going on a diet.   Smokers deny being addicted to tobacco, but in fact, they are.

I admitted having a difficult time following the diet.   They admit giving up cigarettes requires a lot of determination and willpower.

I can't help wanting sweet foods, but I gave up eating anything with sugar in it.   Smokers can't help wanting to smoke, but it's important that they don't give in to the craving.

I avoid eating sweets.   People trying to quit smoking should even avoid breathing smoke from other people's cigarettes.

I quit making cookies on the weekends.   When I quit smoking, I had to quit drinking coffee too.

I practice cooking without sugar.   I practiced relaxing and deep breathing whenever I wanted a cigarette.

This includes eating fruit with my breakfast cereal instead of sugar.   Not smoking includes not being around other smokers.

I can't resist having sweets from time to time, but I will keep on trying to avoid them until I have lost 15 pounds.   I couldn't resist wanting to smoke, but I could resist actually doing so.

Exercise 6

Answers will vary. Possible answers include:

I dislike having homework every night.
I dislike teachers assigning homework over vacations.
I don't mind borrowing money, and if I have enough cash, I don't mind other people borrowing from me.
I enjoy studying grammar.
I enjoy people dropping by my house to visit.
I resent having to work on weekends.
I resent other people expecting me to be a workaholic like them.
We never anticipated having trouble with this unit.
Our teacher never anticipated our having so much trouble with this unit.

Have you ever considered getting cosmetic surgery?

Most American teachers consider a student's asking questions to be a sign that he or she is interested in the lesson.

Is there any way we can delay taking the test?

Please don't delay my entering the university for another semester. I'm running out of money for tuition!

Let's postpone leaving for a while. This party's too much fun!

My mother wanted to postpone my brother's entering kindergarten until he was a little more mature.

Most people appreciate taking a nice hot bath.

Most teachers don't appreciate their students copying each other's homework.

He didn't deny taking the money.

Doctors can't deny some people's needing to smoke, even though they know it's bad for them.

No teacher will excuse cheating on tests.

I can't excuse your behaving so rudely.

Can you imagine being President of the country? How wonderful!

Can you imagine Fred being President of the country? How horrible!

I miss seeing my family.

I miss my mother making me breakfast every morning.

I can tolerate having homework on school nights, but I can't tolerate the teacher making us do homework on weekends.

I can understand leaving the party, but I can't understand your being angry at the hostess. She didn't get involved in our argument.

Exercise 7

Answers will vary. Possible answers include:

1. eating fatty foods; staying up till dawn.
2. being an astronaut; becoming President.
3. reading an English newspaper for 20 minutes each day; doing homework carefully.
4. working on this project; borrowing money from friends.
5. going to another language program; changing my major.
6. other people stealing; being taken advantage of by unscrupulous encyclopedia salespeople.
7. running quickly; kicking the ball accurately.
8. helping students; knowing the material.
9. listening to native speakers; not being afraid to make mistakes.
10. helping with the dishes; not staying too late.

Exercise 8

1. Mary will miss a great deal John's singing a funny song whenever he sees her.
2. Mary doesn't really understand his wanting to become fluent in French.
3. Mary resents his (having applied/applying) to the program without consulting her.
4. She's not looking forward to not having a chance to talk with him every day.
5. John is quite excited about leaving in two weeks.
6. John didn't anticipate needing at least three weeks to get a passport.
7. John wanted to avoid making his departure even later than expected.

Exercise 9

Answers will vary. Possible answers include:

1. is the best thing in the world; requires intelligence and patience.
2. is the dream of every student in this class; means knowing a lot of vocabulary.
3. making friends in this country; having enough money to finish my studies.
4. meeting new people; making mistakes in English class.
5. passing the TOEFL; my not having heard from my family.
6. smoking; working; exercising; doing homework.
7. means getting backaches; happens to everyone.
8. doing homework; eating American food.

Exercise 10

You can correct this exercise in numerous ways, or have students use the page in their texts to write down other verb + gerund/infinitive combinations that they encounter in subsequent reading, listening, and conversation.

Verbs that Take Infinitive Complements			Verbs that Take Gerund Complements		
pattern 1	**pattern 2**	**pattern 3**	**pattern 1**	**pattern 2**	**pattern 3**
appear	advise	expect	can't help	encourage	appreciate
refuse	remind	arrange	keep on	urge	anticipate
seem	persuade	want	recommend	forbid	dislike
agreed	urge	hope	suggest	allow	don't mind
appear	encourage	intend	deny	permit	enjoy
claimed	convince	consent	consider	invites	resent
care	force	ask	admit	cause	consider
deserved	forbid	need	can't help	teach	delay
decided	command		give up		postpone
demanded	order		avoid		appreciate
pretended	allow		quit		deny
hesitated	permit		practice		excuse
offered	invite		include		imagine
refused	trust		resist		miss
seem	cause				tolerate
tended	tell				understand
learned	remind				
neglected	warn				
hopes	teach				
waiting	hire				

Are there some verbs that can be used with both infinitives and gerunds? Which ones are they? Many pattern 2 verbs. See the list above.

Exercise 11

1. to avoid/avoiding
2. talking
3. to pick up
4. barking/to bark
5. smoking
6. to bring
7. playing; to prefer; playing/to play
8. eating

Exercise 12

This is an open-ended exercise:

(1) *time doing nothing in their free time* — gerund complement of *time* (2) *continue to decrease* — infinitive complement of *continue* (Pattern 1)

(3) *requires employees to work* — infinitive complement of *requires* (Pattern 2) (4) *allowed to take* — infinitive complement of *allowed* (Pattern 2) (5) *required to work* — infinitive complement of *required* (Pattern 2); *get to enjoy* — infinitive complement of *get* (Pattern 2) (6) *who spend an average of 42 hours a week working* — gerund complement of *spend time*; *encouraged to take* — infinitive complement of *encouraged* (Pattern 2)

(7) *need to work full-time* — infinitive complement of *need* (Pattern 2) (8) *forced to postpone* — infinitive complement of *forced*; *doing household chores* — gerund complement of *postpone* (9) *need to spend* — infinitive complement of *need* (Pattern 2); *at least one entire day of their weekend doing household chores* — gerund complement of *spend [time]*; *shopping for food, cleaning the house, doing the laundry* — gerund complement of *spend [time]*

(10) *keeping busy* — gerund object of infinitive (11) *to undertake large-scale projects* — infinitive of purpose (see Unit 16); *chance to do* — infinitive complement of *chance*; *painting their houses, repairing their automobiles,…writing grammar books* — gerunds (appositives of *projects*) (12) *arrange for people to work* — infinitive complement of *arrange* (Pattern 2); *to assist ecologists* — infinitive complement of *arrange* (Pattern 2); *with collecting and cataloging plant and animal species* — gerund object of preposition *with* (13) *include going on digs* — gerund object of *include*; *participating in community development projects* — gerund object of *include* (14) *arrange to enroll* — infinitive complement of *arrange* (Pattern 2) (15) *is to take a 300-mile bicycle trip* — infinitive complement of *is*; *to spend a week* — infinitive complement of *is*; *climbing mountains* — gerund complement of *spend [time]*

Exercise 13

(1) pursuing (2) doing (3) making (4) playing (5) singing (6) to keep (7) trying (8) to improve (9) practicing (10) to spend (11) collecting/to collect (12) reading (13) writing (14) to be (15) reading (16) making (17) decorating (18) making (19) carving (20) to fill/filling (21) to stop (22) working on (23) watching (24) playing (25) to be forgotten (26) to be passed on (27) to prefer (28) to be (29) disappearing (30) doing (31) to use

Activities

All the activities in this unit are designed to give students opportunities to use common infinitive and gerund patterns in communicative situations. By having the students write their ideas and responses, any of these activities can be used for testing or diagnostic activities.

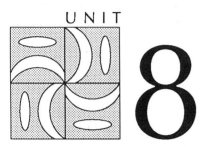

Conjunctions

Task

This Task can be used as a diagnostic by having students write their report to the class. Assign a specific number of sentences describing things that you both like, that neither of you likes, that you like, but not your partner, and that your partner likes, but you don't.

Exercise 1

The conjunctions in this passage have been indicated by bold-face, and the elements that each conjunction connects are listed below.

(1) Matt **and** Jeff   (3) Jeff was from Wisconsin, **and** Matt grew up in Kansas   (4) freedom **or** excitement   (5) that it was a beautiful city, **and** that it was filled with interesting people

(6) surprised **and** delighted; how many things they had in common, **and** how similar their interests were   (7) Jeff liked weightlifting **and** so did Matt   (8) Matt loved opera, **and** Jeff did too   (9) Jeff wasn't entirely comfortable with "big-city" life, **nor** was Matt, **but** neither one missed living in a small town at all   (10) liked dogs **and** wanted to have one for a pet; look for an apartment **and** live together   (11) cheaper **and** more fun

(12) moved in together **and** took up housekeeping   (13) Jeff was very tidy, **but** Matt wasn't   (14) Matt preferred to let the dishes pile up until there were "enough" to bother with, **nor** did he pick up his clothes or keep things neat   (15) one **or** two   (16) Matt liked staying out late every Friday night, **but** Jeff always wanted to get up early on Saturday mornings to clean the house, **and** to finish chores; relaxing **or** playing   (17) **either** have to start making compromises with each other **or** start looking for separate apartments, **and neither** Matt **nor** Jeff   (18) their similarities outweighed their differences, **and** they settled into a life of harmony **and** mutual interests

Exercise 2

1. but/and
2. and
3. or/and
4. or
5. and
6. nor
7. but/and
8. or/and
9. but/and
10. but

Exercise 3

Answers will vary. Possible answers include:

My partner likes Chinese food and Thai food. I like apples and oranges.

My partner likes Chinese food, and I do too. My partner likes Chinese food, and so do I.

I like apples and my partner does too. I like apples and so does my partner.

Both my partner and I like Chinese food. I like both apples and oranges.

I like Chinese food but not Thai food. My partner likes red wine but not white.

My partner likes Thai food, but I don't. I like Mexican food, but my partner doesn't.

My partner doesn't like Mexican food, but I do. I don't like Thai food, but my partner does.

My partner is from either Osaka or Kobe — I can't remember which. She plans to study either electrical or chemical engineering — I can't remember which.

My partner doesn't like tacos or enchiladas. I don't like rap music or opera.

My partner doesn't like rap music, and I don't either. I don't like rap music, and my partner doesn't either.

My partner doesn't like tacos or enchiladas, and neither do I. I don't like rap music, and neither does my partner.

Neither my partner nor I like rap music. I like neither rap music nor opera.

My partner doesn't like rap music, nor do I. I don't like rap music, nor does my partner.

Exercise 4

1. F **2.** A, C, G **3.** B, D **4.** E, H

Exercise 5

1. Canada isn't in South America, and neither is the United States.
2. Canada was once a colony of Great Britain, and so was the United States.
3. Canada is part of the British Commonwealth, but the United States isn't.
4. Most Americans speak English, and most Canadians do too.
5. The Winter Olympics will be held in either Canada or the United States.
6. Both Canada and the United States have democratic governments.
7. Canada hasn't solved the problem of acid rain, and the United States hasn't either.
8. Canada has a large French-speaking minority, but the United States doesn't.

Exercise 6

Answers will vary. Other possible answers have been included:

1. Winters in Northern Canada can be both colder and longer than in the Southern United States.

    Not only can winters in Northern Canada be colder than in the Southern United States, but they can also be longer.

    Winters in Northern Canada can be not only colder, but also longer than in the Southern United States.

2. Either Canada or America might host the Winter Olympics.

3. Canada not only harvests a lot of wheat, but also produces a lot of lumber.

    Canada both harvests a lot of wheat, and produces a lot of lumber.

    Not only does Canada harvest a lot of wheat, but it also produces a lot of lumber.

4. The United States has both a larger population and a larger economic output than Canada.

    The United States has not only a larger population than Canada, but also a larger economic output.

    Not only does the United States have a larger population than Canada, but it also has a larger economic output.

5. Many Canadians speak either English or French as their first language.

6. Neither the United States nor Canada uses Spanish as an official language.

7. Both Canada and the United States were originally settled as British colonies.

   Not only was Canada originally settled as a British colony, but the United States was also.

8. In another 50 years, the largest Spanish-speaking city in North America might be either Mexico City or Los Angeles.

Exercise 7

Answers will vary. Possible answers include:

1. I play both soccer and kickball well.

   Not only do I play soccer well, but also kickball.

   I play soccer well, and also kickball.

2. I like people who are both honest and friendly.

   I like people who are not only honest but also friendly.

3. I don't like people who either don't have a sense of humor or who take themselves too seriously.

   I dislike people who neither have a sense of humor nor take themselves too seriously.

4. I might go to either Mexico or Belize.

   Either I'll go to Mexico, or I'll go to Belize.

5. I like both Alec Baldwin and Bette Midler.

   I like not only Alec Baldwin, but also Bette Midler.

6. English is the language not only of international business, but also of science and technology.

   Studying English improves your chances of getting a good job, and also makes watching American films more enjoyable.

Exercise 8

Answers will vary. Alternative possible answers have been indicated.

1. Jeff likes cleaning, but Matt doesn't.

   Matt doesn't like cleaning, but Jeff does.

2. Jeff might (either) go home for a visit or travel to France on his vacation.

3. Neither Matt nor Jeff plans to return to their hometowns to live.

   Matt doesn't plan to return to his hometown to live, and neither does Jeff. (and Jeff doesn't either.)

   Matt doesn't plan to return to his hometown to live, nor does Jeff.

4. Jeff likes getting up early, but Matt doesn't.

   Matt doesn't like to get up early, but Jeff does.

5. Both Jeff and Matt always wanted to have a dog.

6. Either Matt or Jeff might take the dog to the park this afternoon.

7. Matt likes dancing and meeting friends at discos.

8. Matt and Jeff come from small towns in Kansas and Wisconsin.

Exercise 9

1. Jeff likes to get up early and finish the cleaning on Saturdays.
2. By the time Matt finishes reading the Saturday paper, Jeff has washed the dishes and vacuumed the living room.
3. Jeff cleans the kitchen and living room every Saturday morning.

4. Jeff and Matt come from Kansas and Wisconsin, respectively.

5. Matt vacuums the living and dining rooms every Saturday morning.

Exercise 10

Answers will vary. Possible answers include:

(1) patient, helpful, loving   (2) old, young at heart; old, healthy   (3) has heart problems, doesn't; still works, does; doesn't work, does   (4) a volunteer, not; working, retired   (5) walks five miles every day, swims; volunteers in the library, sings in church   (6) walks, swims; does volunteer work, exercises   (7) like sailing; go shopping on weekends   (8) go sailing on weekends, visit friends; work in the garden, relax with friends on weekends   (9) is a Republican; misses working full-time   (10) like them, respect them; miss them, hope that I will have a similar kind of life when I am their age

Exercise 11

Answers will vary. Possible answers have been listed.

1. (1) My mother doesn't smoke, and neither does my father.
       My mother doesn't smoke, and my father doesn't either.
       My mother doesn't smoke, nor does my father.
       Neither my mother nor father smokes.

   (2) My father gave up smoking years ago, but my mother only quit last year.

   (3) My mother had wanted to quit for a long time, for she knew it was bad for her health.

   (4) She wasn't able to smoke only one or two cigarettes, (and) so she had to give it up entirely.

   (5) My mother sometimes still wants a cigarette, but won't smoke no matter how much she wants to.

   (6) My father is proud of my mother for quitting, and gives her a lot of praise.

2. (1) Canada has a large French-speaking minority, and (but) the United States has a large Spanish-speaking minority.

   (2) Many people in Canada speak French, and (so) all government publications are printed in both languages.

   (3) Canada has two official languages, but the United States discourages the use of languages other than English for official purposes.

   (4) In Canada, the French-speaking minority is concentrated primarily in the Province of Quebec, but in the United States, Spanish-speaking concentrations are found in New York, Florida, New Mexico, and California.

Activities

Activity 1

This is a game. Try first reading the list of Silly Sally's likes and dislikes aloud (using appropriate conjunctions). If students can't guess the secret (and they probably won't), allow them to examine the list in their books. If they still can't guess, you can give away the answer: Silly Sally only likes things that are spelled with double letters.

Activities 2–5

Can all be used as diagnostic or testing activities by having students write their ideas. They can be told to pay special attention to the issues in this chapter: meaning of conjunctions, parallelism, and redundancy. Activity 5 is the most structured of these activities, and therefore adapts most easily to a "testing" focus.

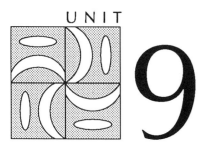

Intensifiers

Task

This task is useful in introducing and underscoring the *very/too* distinction that many students find troublesome.

Exercise 1

Intensifiers are indicated by boldface. The words they modify are indicated by italics.

(1) **very** *dedicated;* **a little** *too serious* (2) **extremely** *hardworking;* **quite** *efficient;* **rather** *competitive;* **not very** *friendly* (4) **really** *too tired* (6) **a bit** *dull;* **really** *interested*

(7) **rather** *easygoing* (8) **fairly** *hard;* **reasonably** *serious* (9) **fairly** *normal* (10) **quite** *active* (11) **rather** *accomplished*

(13) **really** *don't get along* (14) **a little** *lazy;* **insufficiently** *motivated* (15) **rather** *humorless;* **very** *nice* (16) **somewhat** *difficult*

Exercise 2

Answers will vary. Possible answers include:

1. I'm a pretty good baseball player.   I'm a rather good violinist.
2. I'm extremely fond of Scotch.   I really like chocolate.
3. Doing homework can be slightly boring.   Writing grammar books can be a little monotonous.
4. I don't speak Spanish fluently enough.   I don't read fast enough.
5. I eat too much ice cream.   I stay up too late on Saturday nights.
6. I'm a really good musician.   I'm an awfully good dancer.

Exercise 3

Choice of intensifiers will vary. Two possible choices have been indicated.

1. (INFORMAL) More formal: *I'm somewhat/rather sick today.*
2. (FORMAL) More informal: *I'm kind of/pretty confused by all your questions.*
3. (INFORMAL) More formal: *She's quite/extremely unfriendly.*
4. (FORMAL) More informal: *He's really/awfully annoyed about the broken window.*
5. (INFORMAL) More formal: *I'm somewhat/rather busy right now.*
6. (FORMAL) More informal: *It's sort of/pretty hot here, don't you think?*
7. (INFORMAL) More formal: *Peter works very/reasonably hard.*

8. (INFORMAL) More formal: *Denise is rather/quite serious.*
9. (INFORMAL) More formal: *That man is quite/very hard to understand.*

Exercise 4

1. too
2. very
3. too
4. very
5. too
6. very/too; very
7. too/very
8. very
9. very
10. too

Exercise 5

Answers will vary. Possible answers include:

1. It's a bit too expensive.   I'm a little too poor.
2. She's much too serious.   She smiles way too infrequently.
3. I'm really too busy.   I really have too many things to do.
4. It was way too difficult.   It was much too hard.
5. It's a little too bitter.   It's a bit too bitter.

Exercise 6

Answers will vary. Possible answers include:

babies:	They're a little too noisy. They're a bit too messy.
dogs:	They're a bit too dirty. They have too many fleas.
cats:	They're much too independent. They are a little too aloof.
spinach:	It's much too healthy. It tastes much too bitter.
liberals:	They're far too altruistic. They spend way too much money.
workaholics:	They're really too serious. They're a bit too humorless.
diamond necklaces:	They're much too expensive. They're too easy to steal.
weather in the summer:	It's way too hot. It's much too humid.
sports cars:	They are driven way too fast. They're much too expensive.
conservatives:	They're way too rich. They're much too heartless.
studying grammar:	It's much too difficult. It's a little too boring.
being away from my family:	I'm a little too lonely. I get a bit too homesick.
rap music:	It's much too monotonous. It's far too sexist.
police officers:	They're a bit too threatening. I often drive a bit too fast.

Exercise 7

Answers will vary. Possible answers include:

1. She's not too friendly.   She's not very friendly.
2. I didn't quite understand you.   I didn't really understand you.
3. Mary's not too happy with you.   She's not so happy with you.

4. I'm not too fond of Brussels sprouts.   I don't really like Brussels sprouts.
5. You're not being very nice.   Don't be so rude.
6. Mark isn't really a very good cook.   Mark isn't such a great cook.
7. Beth isn't too interested in listening to other people's problems.   She doesn't really enjoy listening to other people's problems.
8. I don't have quite enough room.   There's not too much space.

Exercise 8

There may be a number of ways to correct the problem.

1. INCORRECT — *a little* isn't usually used with *not*.
   The answer isn't a bit complicated.   The answer isn't very complicated.
2. INCORRECT — *so* is not usually used as an intensifier with verbs.
   Learning a language really requires a lot of practice.   Learning a language requires so much practice.
3. INCORRECT — wrong position for the intensifier.
   Henry's quite an intelligent fellow.
4. INCORRECT — wrong position for the intensifier.
   Rebecca isn't tall enough to reach the top shelf.
5. Probably INCORRECT — *too* means excessive.
   I'd like you to meet a friend of mine. He's quite/very intelligent.
6. Possibly CORRECT, but sounds "British."
   It's really/much too hot to even think about going for a run.
7. INCORRECT — *kind of* isn't usually used with *not*.
   Peter's not very busy.   Peter's not so busy.
8. CORRECT.

Activities

Activity 1

This can be done by splitting the class into two groups and appointing a moderator/facilitator for each group. The teacher or a selected student can lead the whole class discussion. Alternatively, it can be done in smaller groups, with the groups themselves reporting on the differences.

Activity 2

The surprises can be reported orally or in written form.

Activity 3

You can eliminate the last step of this activity if you are pressed for time.

Activity 4

Follow the procedure outlined in the Task for Unit 13.

Activity 5

This can be adapted to be used for writing.

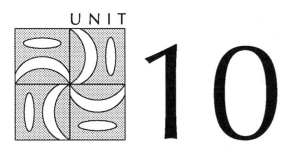

Adjective Modifiers

Task

This adapts well to being used as a diagnostic activity by having the students hand in their written descriptions.

Exercise 1

	Quantifiers	Determiners	Intensifiers	Descriptive Adjectives	Other Modifiers	HEAD NOUN
1.		an		ugly, little		statue
2.	lots of		rather	cute, miniature	circus	animals
3.	one of	your	more	experienced	English	teachers
4.		a	certain	retired	police	officer
5.	some of	that		imported French	goat	cheese
6.	many		very	famous	university	professors
7.	one of	the	most	graceful, amateur	ballroom	dancers
8.		a	wonderfully	relaxing	three-week	vacation

Exercise 2

This is an open-ended exercise.

Category	Adjective							
	1	2	3	4	5	6	7	8
evaluation/ opinion				beautiful			interesting	funky
appearance: *size* *shape* *condition*	small well-polished	big shiny	little fat		round			broken-down
age		new		old	antique		young	old
color		red	brown			black		
origin: *geographical* *material*	Italian leather			Thai silk	wooden	Japanese lacquer	French	
NOUN	shoes	sports car	puppy	pajamas	tea tray	screen	physics professor	Chevrolet

Sentences 3, 5, and 6 do not follow the basic order. Sentence 3 could have *shiny* after *big* also, but highlights *shiny* by putting it first among the adjectives. Likewise, in sentence 5, the author may have wished to emphasize the antique quality of the object and therefore put it first. In sentence 6, material origin precedes geographical origin because the color (*black*) modifies the material (*lacquer*).

Exercise 3

Alternative possible orders are also listed.

(1) strange, new   (2) really useful   (3) bright purple flannel   (4) pretty new French   (5) original plastic   (6) useless, incredibly ugly antique/incredibly ugly, useless antique   (7) plenty of expensive, brand-new/brand-new expensive, bright-colored European   (8) dark, little, overcrowded bedroom   (9) nice, handmade Italian   (10) nice new   (11) poor, old   (12) terrible, frightening/frightening, terrible

Exercise 4

1. INCORRECT ADJECTIVE ORDER: I bought a pretty, old, green vase at the flea market.
2. INCORRECT ADJECTIVE ORDER: He's a brand-new university dormitory resident.
3. INCORRECT ADJECTIVE ORDER: It's a genuine antique old-fashioned black umbrella.
4. CORRECT
5. INCORRECT ADJECTIVE ORDER: Would you like to hear about my exciting summertime vacation plans?

Exercise 5

1. compound noun
2. modified noun
3. compound noun
4. compound noun
5. modified noun
6. compound noun
7. modified noun
8. modified noun
9. modified noun
10. compound noun

Exercise 6

1. a new <u>paper</u> route
2. her newly painted, professionally decorated <u>living</u> room
3. the neighborhood <u>expert</u>
4. the university <u>dormitory</u>
5. no living <u>relatives</u>
6. some paper <u>decorations</u>
7. your <u>antique</u> dealer
8. <u>university</u> students/university <u>students</u>
9. a living <u>wage</u>
10. a genuine antique French <u>teacup</u>

Exercise 7

Answers will vary. Possible answers include:

1. Not an English grammar book. Not one written in Spain.
2. Not a literature book. Not a novel.
3. There's another dog catcher who's tall. He's not the tall one.
4. She's not a repairperson or an executive with the phone company.
5. She doesn't repair Xerox machines or household appliances.
6. He doesn't like thin ones.
7. He only falls in love with ballerinas, not with other kinds of fat people.
8. I don't think she's working anymore.
9. She taught physics, not chemistry.

Activities

Activities 1 and 2

These can be used as diagnostics.

Activities 3 and 4

These games can also be used to test students' mastery of correct word stress.

UNIT 11

Participle Modifiers

Task

Students' understanding of this troublesome difference in meaning can be diagnosed by having the students hand in written responses, and checking to see that students correctly describe **reactions** in reference to past participles and **situations** in reference to present participles.

Exercise 1

This is an open-ended exercise.

1. *adjective* — modifies *expressions*
2. *noun modifier* — modifies *language*
3. *present participle* — modifies *information*
4. *past participle* — modifies *emotions*
5. *adjective* — modifies *basis*
6. *present participle* — modifies *situations*
7. *past participle* — modifies *heart rates*
8. *noun* — modifies *rates*
9. *adverb + past participle* — modifies *individuals*
10. *adverb + past participle* — modifies *immune systems*
11. *adjective* — modifies *expressions*
12. *present participle* — modifies *situation*
13. *present participle* — modifies *feet*
14. *present participle* — modifies *fingers*
15. *past participle* — modifies *indications*
16. *present participle* — modifies *situation*
17. *adjective* — modifies *grin*
18. *adjective* — modifies *language*
19. *present participle* — modifies *message*
20. *past participle* — modifies *eye contact*
21. *past participle* — modifies *body language*
22. *adjective* — modifies *word*

Exercise 2

1. confused; confusing
2. disappointing; disappointed
3. Frightened; Frightening
4. satisfying; satisfied
5. interested; interesting

Exercise 3

1. exciting
2. increased
3. embarrassing
4. unintended
5. depressing/seriously depressing

6. depressed/seriously depressed
7. puzzling
8. puzzled

Exercise 4

1. a stunt that defies death
2. a cake that was bought in a store
3. an expert that is renowned all over the world
4. a fact that boggles the mind
5. a sweater that was made by hand
6. a machine that reduces weight
7. a maneuver that saves face
8. an employee who is well-trained
9. a kitten that is starved for love
10. an economic policy that causes us to tighten our belts

Exercise 5

Answers will vary. Possible answers include:

1. Grammar class is never boring.
   Nobody likes boring people.
2. The Republicans seemed enormously self-satisfied at their convention.
   Charley thinks he's God's gift to women. He's the most self-satisfied person I've ever met.
3. The police caught a very surprised thief in their sting operation.
   I wasn't at all surprised to hear the news.
4. I saw an amazing sight yesterday.
   Some EFL teachers have an amazing lack of cross-cultural knowledge or sensitivity.
5. Psychiatrists are more commonly treating deeply depressed patients with drugs instead of psychotherapy.
   Deeply depressed people sometimes show symptoms of physical illness, such as headaches or nausea.
6. Bungee-jumping is an exhilarating activity.
   We had an exhilarating time water-skiing.
7. We're very worried about the deficit.
   She's worried about Tom's remarks.
8. Most modern-thinking people realize that America is becoming a multicultural society.
   Modern-thinking people usually don't believe in ghosts or witches.
9. Disinterested students rarely make much effort to do well.
   He dismissed us with a disinterested wave of his hand.
10. Gladys has a very irritating habit of interrupting people in conversations.
    Irritating people should be told about their annoying behavior.

Exercise 6

(1) nonspoken (2) confusing (3) annoyed (4) bored (5) disinterested (6) uninvolved (7) interesting (8) involving (9) actively engaged (10) confused (11) embarrassed (12) confused (13) worried (14) teacher-challenging (15) slightly insulting (16) surprised (17) sometimes mistaken

Exercise 7

This is an open-ended exercise. Note that "breaking that arm's length bubble" in sentence 5 is a gerund, not a participle.

(1) *frequently mentioned by researchers discussing cross-cultural differences* — that is frequently mentioned by researchers who are discussing cross-cultural differences (2) *maintained between people engaged in different kinds of conversation* — which is maintained between people who are engaged in different kinds of conversation

(3) *carrying on polite "social" conversations* — who are carrying on polite "social" conversations (4) *having a more "intimate" relationship* — who have/are having a more "intimate" relationship (5) No participial adjectival phrase

(6) *raised in Latin societies* — who were raised in Latin societies (7) No participial phrase

Activities

Activity 1

Can be used as diagnostic or testing activity.

Activities 4 and 5

May be used in conjunction with discussing the information on silent language presented in Exercises 1, 6, and 7. This also provides an excellent opportunity for teachers to outline explicitly what is meant by "classroom participation" in an American classroom.

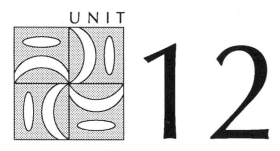

Comparatives

Task

Written responses to the discussion questions about rich countries versus poor countries, or comparative statements about the statistics on the countries listed are both good ways to assess whether or not students need work on comparatives.

Exercise 1

Answers will vary. Possible answers include:

(a) The population of the United States is **much larger than** the population of Canada.

The area of Canada is **somewhat larger than** the area of the United States.

(b) The United States is **considerably more populous** than Canada.

Catholics in Canada are **proportionally more numerous than** in the United States.

(c) Canada's population is growing **a bit more rapidly than** that of the United States.

People in the United States are living **somewhat more prosperously than** people in Canada.

(d) Winters in Canada are just **as cold as** winters in the northern United States.

Most Canadians love apple pie **as sincerely as** Americans.

(e) America's literacy rate is **almost as high as** Canada's.

The population of the United States is increasing **nearly as quickly as** Canada's.

(f) The literacy rate of the United States is **not quite as high as** Canada's.

The area of the United States is **not quite as large as** that of Canada.

(g) The population of the United States is **not** increasing **quite as quickly as** Canada's.

Canada **is not** populated **nearly as densely as** the United States.

(h) The United States population is growing **a little less quickly than** that of Canada.

Canadians seem to teach reading **a little more effectively** than Americans.

(i) The people of Canada are **somewhat less prosperous than** the people of the United States.

The Jewish population in Canada is **considerably less numerous than** the Jewish population in the United States.

Exercise 2

This is an open-ended exercise. Students should be able to (1) correctly identify what is being compared (since in some sentences, one of the elements is implied rather than directly stated), and (2) correctly interpret the comparative relationship. The exact wording of the identified elements does not need to correspond precisely to the wording used in the answers below.

(1) Although (a) the population of Bangladesh is slightly larger than that of Pakistan, (b) its land area is considerably smaller. (2) This means that the (a) population density of Pakistan is not nearly as great as that of Bangladesh, and as a result, (b) the general standard of living is substantially higher. (3) Although (a) the population of Bangladesh is not growing quite as quickly as Pakistan's, (b) its GNP is quite a bit lower, and as a result, it will be a very long time before the (c) standard of living for Bangladeshis becomes as high as for Pakistanis. (4) While (a) educational development is almost as high in Bangladesh as in Pakistan, (b) economic development is substantially lower, and (c) people in Bangladesh are generally less prosperous.

1. (a) X = population of Bangladesh; Y = population of Pakistan
   $X > Y$ (small difference)
   (b) X = land area of Bangladesh; Y = land area of Pakistan
   $X < Y$ (large difference)
2. (a) X = population density of Pakistan; Y = population density (that) of Bangladesh
   $X < Y$ (large difference)
   (b) X = standard of living of Pakistan; Y = standard of living of Bangladesh
   $X > Y$ (large difference)
3. (a) X = population of Bangladesh; Y = Pakistan's (population)
   $X < Y$ (small difference)
   (b) X = Bangladesh's GNP; Y = Pakistan's GNP
   $X < Y$ (large difference)
   (c) X = standard of living for Bangladeshis; Y = standard of living for Pakistanis
   $X < Y$ (It will be a long time before X = Y.)
4. (a) X = educational development in Bangladesh; Y = educational development in Pakistan
   $X < Y$ (small difference)
   (b) X = economic development in Bangladesh; Y = economic development in Pakistan
   $X < Y$ (large difference)
   (c) X = people in Bangladesh; Y = (people in Pakistan — not directly stated)
   $X < Y$ (amount of difference not directly stated)

Exercise 3

Answers will vary. Possible answers include:

1. The GNP of Bangladesh is not nearly as high as the GNP of Pakistan.
2. The GNP of Pakistan is substantially higher than that of Bangladesh.
3. The literacy rate in Pakistan is slightly higher than it is in Bangladesh.
4. The literacy rate in Bangladesh is not quite as high as it is in Pakistan.
5. The population is growing somewhat less quickly in Bangladesh than it is in Pakistan.
6. The population in Pakistan is growing slightly more quickly than it is in Bangladesh.
7. The population of Bangladesh is somewhat larger than that of Pakistan.
8. The population of Pakistan is not quite as large as that of Bangladesh.
9. The population is much denser in Bangladesh than it is in Pakistan.
10. The population of Pakistan is not nearly as dense as that of Bangladesh.

Exercise 4

Answers will vary. Possible answers include:

- **(a)** Canada has **a bit more land area than** the United States.
- **(b)** The United States has **many more people than** Canada does.
- **(c)** Southern Canada has **as many cold weeks as** the Northern United States does.
- **(d)** Southern Canada has **as much snowfall as** the Northern United States does.
- **(e)** The United States has **almost as many square miles as** Canada does.
  The United States has **almost as much land area as** Canada does.
- **(f)** The United States **doesn't have proportionally quite the percentage of Catholics that** Canada has.
- **(g)** The United States **doesn't have quite as much land area as** Canada.
- **(h)** Canada has **substantially fewer Jews than** the United States.
- **(i)** Canada has **much less population density than** the United States.

Exercise 5

See comments for Exercise 2.

(1) Although (a) <u>Bangladesh has somewhat more people than Pakistan</u>, (b) <u>it has considerably less land area</u>. (2) This means that (a) <u>Pakistan does not have nearly as many people per square mile as Bangladesh does</u>, and as a result, there is (b) <u>much less pressure</u> on economic infrastructure, roads, water supply, and so on. (3) As a rule, (a) <u>people in Bangladesh have somewhat fewer opportunities for economic progress than people in Pakistan</u>. (4) (a) <u>Bangladesh has just about as many literate people as Pakistan</u>, but (b) <u>it has fewer people living above the poverty line</u>, and so (c) <u>there is somewhat less political and economic stability in Bangladesh than there is in Pakistan</u>. (5) However, (a) <u>Pakistan has more regional ethnic groups than Bangladesh</u>, and (b) <u>there are more incidents of ethnic unrest in Pakistan than there are in Bangladesh</u>. (6) Thus, in the political arena overall, <u>Bangladesh has fewer overt conflicts than Pakistan</u>.

1. (a) X = Bangladesh has (a number of) people. Y = Pakistan does too.
     $X > Y$ (small or medium difference)
   (b) X = Bangladesh has (an amount of) land area. Y = Pakistan does too.
     $X < Y$ (large difference)
2. (a) X = Pakistan has (a number of) people per square mile. Y = Bangladesh does too.
     $X < Y$ (large difference)
   (b) X = pressure on the economic infrastructure, etc., in Pakistan. Y = pressure on the economic infrastructure, etc., in Bangladesh.
     $X < Y$ (large difference)
3. (a) X = people in Bangladesh have some opportunities for economic progress. Y = people in Pakistan do too.
     $X < Y$ (small or medium difference)
4. (a) X = Bangladesh has (a number of) literate people. Y = Pakistan does too.
     $X < Y$ (very small difference) or $X = Y$
   (b) X = Bangladesh has (a number of) people living above the poverty line. Y = Pakistan does too.
     $X < Y$ (amount of difference not stated)
   (c) X = there is (a certain amount of) political and economic stability in Bangladesh. Y = there is (a certain amount of) political and economic stability in Pakistan.
     $X < Y$ (a small or medium difference)
5. (a) X = Pakistan has (a number of) regional ethnic groups. Y = Bangladesh does too.
     $X > Y$ (amount of difference not stated)

(b) *X* = incidents of ethnic unrest in Pakistan. *Y* = incidents of ethnic unrest in Bangladesh.
   X > *Y* (amount of difference not stated)

(c) *X* = overt political conflicts in Bangladesh. *Y* = overt political conflicts in Pakistan.
   X < *Y* (amount of difference not stated)

Exercise 6

Answers will vary. Possible answers include:

1. Bangladesh has somewhat fewer regional ethnic groups than Pakistan.
   Bangladesh doesn't have quite as many regional ethnic groups as Pakistan.
2. Pakistan has (quite a few/significantly) more regional languages than Bangladesh does.
3. Bangladesh has more people than Pakistan does.
4. Pakistan has slightly fewer literate people than Bangladesh does.
   Pakistan doesn't have quite as many literate people as Bangladesh.
5. Bangladesh has significantly more Hindu citizens than Pakistan does.
   Bangladesh has a larger number of Hindu citizens than Pakistan.
6. Pakistan has considerably fewer Hindu citizens than Bangladesh.
   Pakistan doesn't have nearly as many Hindu citizens as Bangladesh.

Exercise 7

Answers will vary. (See Exercise 9 for other possible alternatives.) Possible answers include:

1. **population:** Bangladesh has a somewhat larger population than Pakistan.
2. **growth rate:** Bangladesh doesn't have quite as high a population growth rate as Pakistan.
3. **literacy:** Bangladesh has almost as many literate people as Pakistan.
4. **economic development:** Bangladesh doesn't have as much economic development as Pakistan.
5. **ethnic groups:** Bangladesh has significantly fewer regional ethnic groups than Pakistan.
6. **level of prosperity:** Bangladesh doesn't have nearly the same level of prosperity as Pakistan.

Exercise 8

Answers will vary. (See Exercise 9 for other possible alternatives.) Possible answers include:

1. **land area:** The United States doesn't have quite as much land area as Canada.
2. **population growth rate:** The United States has a slightly lower growth rate than Canada.
3. **percentage of Protestants:** The United States has a higher percentage of Protestants than Canada does.
4. **official languages of the two countries:** The United States doesn't have as many official languages as Canada.
5. **literacy rate:** The United States doesn't have quite as high a literacy rate as Canada.
6. **population density:** The United States has a much higher population density than Canada.
7. **per capita income:** People in the United States have somewhat more per capita income than people in Canada do.
8. **GNP:** The United States has a substantially larger GNP than Canada.
9. **overall population:** The United States has a great many more people than Canada.

Exercise 9

Answers will vary. Sample answers include:

BANGLADESH/PAKISTAN

1. population: Pakistan has somewhat fewer people than Bangladesh.
2. growth rate: Pakistan has a slightly higher population growth rate than Bangladesh.
3. literacy: Pakistan has a slightly higher literacy rate than Bangladesh.
4. economic development: Pakistan has more economic development than Pakistan does.
5. ethnic groups: Pakistan has significantly more regional ethnic groups than Bangladesh.
6. level of prosperity: Pakistan has a considerably higher level of prosperity than Bangladesh.

UNITED STATES/CANADA

1. land area: Canada has slightly more land area than the United States.
2. population growth rate: Canada has a slightly higher population growth rate than Canada.
3. percentage of Protestants: Canada doesn't have as many Protestants as the United States does.
4. official languages of the two countries: Canada has more official languages than the United States.
5. literacy rate: Canada has a slightly higher number of literate people than the United States.
6. population density: Canada has a significantly lower population density than the United States.
7. per capita income: People in Canada have somewhat less per capita income than people in the United States.
8. GNP: Canada doesn't have nearly as large a GNP as the United States does.
9. overall population: Canada doesn't have nearly as many people as the United States does.

Exercise 10

See comments for Exercise 2.

(1) *English speakers don't all speak quite the same kind of English*
   a) kinds of English; b) similar

(2) *Things like vocabulary and pronunciation are often substantially different*
   a) things like vocabulary and pronunciation; b) different

(5) *The pronunciation features of these two "Englishes" are quite different*
   a) pronunciation features of these two Englishes; b) different

(6) *British English is substantially different from American English*
   a) British English/American English; b) (quite) different

(8) *many people think that Canadian and American varieties of English are exactly the same…and not all words are pronounced alike*
   a) Canadian and American varieties of English; b) similar

(9) *In America the vowel sound in the word* out *is pronounced differently from that in* boot
   a) the pronunciation of the vowel sound in *out* and *boot*; b) different

(10) shout *basically like* shoot
   a) the pronunciation of *shout* and *shoot*; b) very similar/almost the same

(11) *To most people, Canadian English and American English seem very much alike*
   a) Canadian English and American English; b) very similar/almost the same

(12) *Americans speak the language differently from their northern neighbors*
   a) the ways Americans and Canadians speak the language; b) different

Exercise 11

Answers will vary. Possible answers include:

- **a) identical:** Canada had the same colonial government as the United States did.

  Both the United States and Canada once had the same colonial government.

- **b) similar:** Canada has almost the same land area and population growth rate as the United States does.

  Both Canada and the United States have almost the same land area and population growth rate.

- **c) somewhat different:** The United States doesn't have quite the same literacy rate as Canada.

  Canada and the United States don't have quite the same literacy rates.

- **d) very different:** The United States has quite a different official language policy than Canada.

  Canada and the United States have quite different official language policies.

Exercise 12

Answers will vary. Possible answers include:

- **a) identical:** Bangladesh had the same colonial government as Pakistan did.

  Both Bangladesh and Pakistan once had the same colonial government.

- **b) similar:** Bangladesh has almost the same literacy rate as Pakistan.

  Bangladesh and Pakistan have almost the same literacy rate.

- **c) somewhat different:** The percentage of Muslim citizens in Bangladesh is somewhat different than it is in Pakistan.

  The percentage of Muslim citizens in Bangladesh and Pakistan is somewhat different.

- **d) very different:** The ethnic groups in Bangladesh are quite different from those in Pakistan.

  The ethnic groups in Bangladesh and Pakistan are quite different.

Exercise 13

Answers will vary. This exercise may be omitted or used as the topic for brief oral presentations in place of the Activities.

Exercise 14

1. British and American speakers of English use slang expressions quite differently.
2. No two countries speak a common language exactly the same.
3. Spanish in Spain is spoken differently from Spanish in Latin America.
4. The word *color* is not spelled alike in Britain and in America.
5. Many Canadians pronounce *shout* basically the same as *shoot*.
6. The grammar in regional varieties of English is all basically alike.

Exercise 15

See comments for Exercise 2.

(1) *languages that have somewhat the same linguistic structure*
   a) groups of languages/linguistic structure
   b) somewhat similar
   c) *somewhat*

(3) *cultures that have more or less the same basic values, attitudes, and beliefs*
   a) groups of cultures/values, attitudes, and beliefs
   b) very similar
   c) *more or less the same*

(4) *one "European" culture...has many of the same basic characteristics as any other European culture*
   a) European cultures/basic characteristics
   b) very similar/almost identical
   c) *the same basic characteristics*

(5) *Countries in Latin America are quite different from each other*
   a) customs and social structures of countries in Latin America
   b) very different
   c) *quite different*

(6) *people from Colombia will probably think more like people from Venezuela than like people from Nepal*
   a) people from Colombia and Venezuela/thinking
   b) somewhat similar
   c) *will think more like people from Venezuela than like people from Nepal*

(7) *a Nepalese and an Indian will be more alike than a Nepalese and a Viennese*
   a) a Nepalese and an Indian
   b) somewhat similar
   c) *more alike than a Nepalese and a Viennese*

(8) *No culture has exactly the same set of values as another culture*
   a) all cultures/sets of values
   b) very different
   c) *no culture has exactly the same...*

(9) *a number of factors that make a particular culture more like one culture than another one*
   a) a particular culture/one culture
   b) somewhat similar
   c) *more like one culture than another*

(11) *People who have the same religion also tend to have the same general "world view" and moral values*
   a) religion/world view and moral values
   b) the same
   c) *the same religion...the same "world view" and moral values*

(12) *Their specific beliefs and practices may not be exactly alike*
   a) beliefs and practices
   b) different
   c) *not...exactly alike*

(13) *one group of followers may be quite different from those of another group*
   a) one group of followers/another group
   b) very different
   c) *quite different*

(15) *Sunni Muslims and Shi'ite Muslims have some fundamentally different ideas*
   a) Sunni and Shi'ite Muslims/ideas
   b) different
   c) *fundamentally different*

   view the world quite differently from Buddhists
   a) Muslims and Buddhists/view the world
   b) very different
   c) *quite differently*

(16) *Roman Catholics worship somewhat differently from Protestants*
   a) Roman Catholic and Protestants/worship
   b) somewhat different
   c) *somewhat differently*

   both groups observe Christmas and Easter in very much the same way
   a) Roman Catholic and Protestants/observing Christmas and Easter
   b) very similar
   c) *in very much the same way*

(18) *Cultures that have a shared historical background tend to have somewhat the same outlook on the world*
   a) cultures with a shared historical background/outlook on the world
   b) similar
   c) *somewhat the same*

(20) *the differences between cultures can sometimes be more important than the similarities*
   a) cultural differences and similarities/importance
   b) different
   c) *more important than*

(22) *their economic and political interests may be alike*
   a) economic and political interests
   b) same
   c) *alike*

   cultures that think quite differently from one another may choose to act quite differently as well
   a) cultures/thinking and acting
   b) very different
   c) *quite differently*

(23) *political boundaries change much more frequently and more rapidly than cultural boundaries*
   a) political and cultural boundaries/change
   b) different
   c) *more frequently and more rapidly*

Exercise 16

1. Sunni Muslims follow the same five basic precepts of Islam **as** Shi'ite Muslims do.
2. Catholic Christians regard the Pope differently **from** Protestant Christians.
3. Mahayana Buddhists don't put the same emphasis on being a monk as Theravada Buddhists **(do)**.
4. The social values of Germany are quite different **from those of** Italy.

5. Many people in Washington, D.C., have a different attitude toward the role of the federal government **from** many people in San Francisco.
6. The Civil War in the United States was caused in large part by the fact that people in the North felt differently on the subject of slavery **from** people in the South.
7. The Indians of Peru speak almost the same language **as** the Indians in Bolivia **(do)**.
8. The English spoken in New Zealand is slightly different **from** that spoken in Australia.

Exercise 17

1. *like* expresses a comparative statement.
2. *like* expresses "for example" or "such as."
3. *as* expresses a comparative statement.
4. *as* expresses a simile.
5. First sentence: *like* informal usage for *as if*. Second sentence: The first *like* is a verb, the second *like* is a comparative.
6. *like* expresses a comparative statement.
7. *like* expresses a comparative statement.
8. *like* expresses a comparative statement.
9. *like* — informal usage for *as if* or *that*
10. The first *like* — informal usage for *as if* or *that*; the second *like* expresses a comparative statement.
11. *like* expresses a comparative statement.
12. *like* — informal usage for *as if* (simile)
13. *like* — informal usage for *as if* (simile)
14. *like* expresses a simile.

Activities

Activity 1

This can be used as an additional exercise to practice the patterns presented in Focus 3 and 4.

Activity 2

You may wish to lead the discussion on generic differences yourself.

Activity 3

This activity can also be done in small groups. Students may need some additional guidance and discussion on the differences between *stereotypes* and *generalizations*. In trying to state the latter, they have occasionally been known to blunder into the former. This, of course, in certain politically correct circles, is considered to be a form of blasphemy and has been known to induce palpitations in certain highly sensitive individuals. Teachers with particularly delicate constitutions (lacking first amendments, in particular) should probably choose another activity from this unit.

Activity 4

Students could also compare cities, styles of cooking, or anything else.

Logical Connectors

Task

The procedure outlined here can be used with any written assignment.

Exercise 1

(1) **and** — *form:* coordinator; *meaning:* addition
    since — *form:* subordinator; *meaning:* reason
(2) **although** — *form:* subordinator; *meaning:* concession
(3) **first** — *form:* sentence adverbial; *meaning:* sequence
(4) **because** — *form:* subordinator; *meaning:* reason
(5) **also** — *form:* sentence adverbial; *meaning:* addition
(6) **although** — *form:* subordinator; *meaning:* concession
    nevertheless — *form:* sentence adverbial; *meaning:* concession
(7) **eventually** — *form:* sentence adverbial; *meaning:* sequence
    but — *form:* coordinator; *meaning:* contrast
    even though — *form:* subordinator; *meaning:* concession
(8) **in fact** — *form:* sentence adverbial; *meaning:* emphasis
(9) **because** — *form:* subordinator; *meaning:* reason
(10) **indeed** — *form:* sentence adverbial; *meaning:* emphasis
    actually — *form:* sentence adverbial; *meaning:* emphasis
(11) **as a result** — *form:* sentence adverbial; *meaning:* result
(12) **soon** — *form:* sentence adverbial; *meaning:* sequence (not listed in chart)
(13) **because** — *form:* subordinator; *meaning:* reason
(14) **even though** — *form:* subordinator; *meaning:* concession
(15) **because of** — *form:* subordinator; *meaning:* reason (not listed in chart) (not used with independent clauses) (Focus 5)
    so that — *form:* subordinator; *meaning:* purpose
(17) **first** — *form:* sentence adverbial; *meaning:* sequence
    and — *form:* coordinator; *meaning:* addition
(18) **furthermore** — *form:* sentence adverbial; *meaning:* emphasis
(19) **as a result of** — *form:* subordinator; *meaning:* result (not used with independent clauses) (Focus 5)
(20) **also** — *form:* sentence adverbial; *meaning:* addition
(21) **and** — *form:* coordinator; *meaning:* addition
    as a result — *form:* sentence adverbial; *meaning:* result

(22) **In spite of the fact that** — *form: subordinator; meaning: concession (not listed on the chart)*

(23) **moreover** — *form: sentence adverbial; meaning: emphasis (not listed on the chart)*

Exercise 2

(1) on the other hand   (2) But/However   (3) Moreover   (4) As a result   (5) and/so   (6) under such circumstances   (7) Even though/Consequently   (8) no connector/but   (9) however/on the other hand,   (10) In addition/Besides   (11) However

Exercise 3

Answers will vary. Possible answers include:

1. In addition to missing his family, Bambang also missed things about Indonesia.
   …Bambang became tired of speaking English all the time.
2. In spite of sometimes still missing his family, Bambang doesn't feel as depressed as before.
   …Bambang no longer wants to return home before he finishes his studies.
3. Before he talked to his advisor about culture shock, he was thinking about returning home.
   …he wasn't aware of it.
4. Bambang now understands that his depression was the result of culture shock. Because of this, he feels better about his experience here.
   …he no longer is thinking about going home.
5. Bambang sometimes does poorly on tests, even though he studies hard.
   …he is intelligent and hardworking.
6. Bambang sometimes does poorly on tests, in spite of studying hard.
   …being intelligent and hardworking.
7. Canada has an official policy of bilingualism. The United States, however, doesn't.
   …actually discourages the use of other languages besides English.
8. Canada has an official policy of bilingualism. Consequently, all students study both languages in school.
   …all official government activities are conducted in both languages.
9. As a result of Canada's official policy of bilingualism, all students study both languages in school.
   …all official government activities are conducted in both languages.
10. Canada's French-speaking minority is concentrated in a particular part of the country. Consequently there's a lot of support for the policy there.
    …the policy isn't as popular with people in other parts of the country.
11. Canada's French-speaking minority is concentrated in a particular part of the country. Nevertheless all students study both languages in school.
    …all official government activities are conducted in both languages.
12. Because all government business is conducted in both languages, all students study both languages in school.
    …Canada can be said to have two official languages.

Exercise 4

Answers will vary. Possible answers include:

1. I still often feel homesick, and I miss my family.

   I still often feel homesick. **In addition,** I miss my family.

2. Everything was strange. **Nevertheless,** I enjoyed the new experiences.

   Everything was strange, but I enjoyed the new experiences **nevertheless.**

3. The differences weren't interesting. **They** were boring.

   The differences weren't interesting. **In fact,** they were boring.

4. I learned that every person has this kind of experience, and **that** it can't be avoided.

   I learned that every person has this kind of experience. **Not only that,** it can't be avoided.

5. This was good advice, **and,** as a result, my culture shock became less. **However, in spite of this,** I still miss my life in Indonesia.

   This was good advice. As a result, my culture shock became less, **but,** in spite of this, I still miss my life in Indonesia.

Exercise 5

While students should be able to identify the specific problem, the ways used to correct the problem may vary.

1. Wrong meaning for the logical connector. The situation requires additive rather than contrastive meaning.

   Every person has experience with culture shock, and I am no exception.

2. Too many logical connectors.

   Even though I studied, my grades weren't good.

   I studied. However, my grades weren't good.

3. *Also* is not needed. Wrong meaning for *nevertheless* and *besides*.

   In Canada, all official government activities are conducted in both French and English. Under such circumstances, students study both languages in school. In the United States, on the other hand, there is no official bilingual policy in government operations. In fact, some local governments have policies that prohibit the use of any language other than English for official business.

Exercise 6

While students should be able to identify the specific problem, the ways used to correct the problem may vary.

1. *Although* is a subordinating conjunction, and can't be used with an independent clause.

   Although I have lived in the United States for almost one year, I often feel homesick and miss my family.

2. *Even though* is a subordinating conjunction, and can't be used with an independent clause.

   Even though I was used to them, I still wasn't comfortable.

3. *However* and *for example* are sentence adverbials. They should be followed by commas, and be used with independent clauses.

   However, I began to miss things in Indonesia. For example, I missed the food, my friends, and the warm climate.

4. *In addition to* must be used with a noun phrase or a gerund phrase, not with a clause.

   In addition to telling me about culture shock, my advisor suggested that I should be patient.

Activities

Activity 1

This basic format can be used with any of the written activities in this book, either for diagnosis or testing. For this particular Activity, mark problems with logical connectors either by using the system in the Task, or by highlighting/circling/underlining problematic sentences.

Activity 2 represents a logical topic for Activity 1.

Activity 3

This can be done as a small-group discussion. You may have already noticed some of these words in previous samples of student writing.

Activity 4

Answers will vary. Possible interpretations include:

Indian food is spicy, and I love it.	(That's why I love it.)
Indian food is spicy, but I love it.	(Even so, I love it anyway.)
Indian food is spicy, so I love it.	(That's why I love it.)
Although Indian food is spicy, I love it. *Although I love Indian food, it's spicy.*	There is a difference in emphasis. In the first sentence, the fact that I love Indian food is the most important. In the second sentence, the fact that Indian food is spicy is the most important.
Not only is Indian food spicy, but I also love it.	(The two ideas don't share a strong logical cause-and-effect relationship.)
Because Indian food is spicy, I love it.	(The emphasis is on the cause-and-effect relationship.)
I love Indian food, and it is spicy.	(The logical connector doesn't give information about the way these two ideas are related. Most teachers would consider this to be a run-on sentence.)
I love Indian food, so it is spicy.	(This logical connector indicates result rather than cause.)
Since I love Indian food, it is spicy.	(This logical connector indicates result rather than cause.)

Activity 5

This is designed to be an "open-ended" activity.

UNIT 14

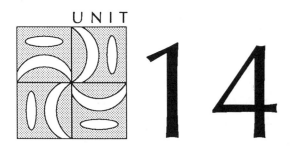

Degree Complements
Too/Enough...To and *So/Such...That*

Task

Other examples of environmental changes are the proliferation of kudzu in the southern United States, the introduction of a freshwater mussel into the Great Lakes, and the introduction of bass into fishing waters in California (which decimated the native trout).

Exercise 1

PASSAGE 1

(1) **Statement of degree:** Denise is very rushed at work these days.
 Result: She doesn't have any free time.

(2) **Statement of degree:** She has very little energy at the end of the workday.
 Result: She can't pursue any hobbies.

(3) **Statement of degree:** She's very busy.
 Result: She hasn't made any close friends.

(4) **Statement of degree:** She always says that there's a lot going on at work.
 Result: She can't take a vacation right now.

(5) no degree complements in this sentence

(6) **Statement of degree:** Her secretary types rather slowly.
 Result: She can't keep up with all the letters Denise writes.

(7) **Statement of degree:** Peter works moderately hard.
 Result: He has avoided being fired.

(8) **Statement of degree:** He isn't excessively dedicated to his job.
 Result: He isn't willing to sacrifice everything else in order to get ahead.

(9) **Statement of degree:** He loves his family a lot.
 Result: He has made their needs his most important priority.

(10) **Statement of degree:** He's just not very competitive about his job.
 Result: Denise doesn't consider him a threat to her authority.

PASSAGE 2

(1) **Statement of degree:** In the second half of the twentieth century, there has been a rapid growth in population.
 Result: Many countries have started to develop lands that only a few years ago were uninhabited, dense, tropical rain forest.

64

(2) **Statement of degree:** The need for lumber for export and land for agriculture has become very great.
    Result: Literally hundreds of square miles of tropical rain forest are now disappearing every day.
(3) no degree complements in this sentence
(4) **Statement of degree:** There is very little fertility in the soil of most tropical areas once the forests have been cut.
    Result: The jungle won't grow back again.
(5) **Statement of degree:** The problem has gotten serious.
    Result: The United Nations has become involved.
(6) no degree complements in this sentence
(7) **Statement of degree:** Rain forests contain a great many plants with possible medical uses.
    Result: Scientists are worried that many valuable species will be destroyed before we can find out how useful they are.
(8) **Statement of degree:** The destruction of the rain forests is extremely important.
    Result: It can't be ignored.
(9) no degree complements in this sentence
(10) **Statement of degree:** Rain forests are disappearing very quickly.
    Result: Scientists are afraid that this may already be causing changes in the atmosphere and weather.
(11) **Statement of degree:** There are signs that it may already be very late.
    Result: We might not be able to stop this process of global warming and climatic change.

Exercise 2

1. b **2.** b **3.** a **4.** b

Exercise 3

Answers will vary. Possible answers include:

1. They are old enough to drive.
   They're too young to drive.
2. They are old enough to be given some financial responsibility.
   They're too young to be given any financial responsibility.
3. They're old enough to fall in love.
   They're too young to fall in love.
4. They're old enough to be allowed to choose what classes they want to take.
   They're too young to be allowed to choose what classes they want to take.
5. They're old enough for teachers to talk to them as adults.
   They're too young for teachers to talk to them as adults.
6. They're old enough to be able to buy alcohol or cigarettes.
   They're too young to be able to buy alcohol or cigarettes.
7. They're old enough for their parents to let them live in their own apartments.
   They're too young for their parents to let them live in their own apartments.

8. They're old enough for the law to treat them as adults.
   They're too young for the law to treat them as adults.
9. They're old enough to be police officers or soldiers.
   They're not old enough to be police officers or soldiers.
10. They're old enough for society to give them total freedom.
    They're too young to be given total freedom.

Exercise 4

1. Denise has too many responsibilities to take a vacation right now.
2. The pace of work is too hectic for Denise to do her best work.
3. Denise's secretary types too slowly for Denise to catch up on her correspondence.
4. Mr. Green hasn't assigned Denise enough additional clerical support for her to meet the contract deadline.
5. Denise is too proud to ask her boss for more help.
6. Denise has behaved rudely to Peter too often for him to offer to help her with the contract.
7. There is always enough free time for Peter to spend on his friends, his music, and his family.
8. Peter plays the clarinet well enough to be a professional musician.
9. He doesn't like Denise enough to help her meet her contract deadline.
10. Work is not important enough for Peter to make it the focus of his life.

Exercise 5

Answers will vary. Possible answers include:

1. No, I'm too young to have any.   No, I'm not old enough to have any.
2. No, that's too far to walk.   No, that's not enough time to walk that far.
3. No, that's too expensive.
4. No, they're not intelligent enough to read.   No, they're too stupid.
5. No, it's too cold in Russia for banana trees to grow wild.   No, Russia isn't hot enough for banana trees to grow wild.
6. No, a piano is too heavy for one person to lift.   No, one person isn't strong enough to lift a grand piano.
7. No, that isn't enough time to learn to speak English fluently.   No, that's too little time to learn to speak English fluently.
8. No, she's too old to still have babies.   No, she's no longer young/strong enough to have babies.
9. No, I was too young to remember.   That was too long ago for me to remember.   I wasn't old enough to remember.
10. No, that's too many for me to eat.   I would never be hungry enough to be able to eat 50 hamburgers in a single meal.

Four other "stupid" questions: Can you fly? Can you run faster than a train? Is one penny a suitable tip for a waiter? Is 37 children a good number for a single mother to raise?

Exercise 6

Answers will vary. Possible answers include:

1. Enough to feed, clothe, and educate your children.
   Enough to take a European vacation every year.
2. I speak it well enough to understand most of what I hear and read.
   I don't speak it well enough yet to pass the TOEFL.
3. When they are old enough to work full-time.
   When they have enough money to live by themselves.
4. When they are old enough to make mature decisions.
   When they are too old to want to play around anymore.
5. Fast enough to keep up with the rest of the traffic.
   Slowly enough to obey the speed limit.
6. When you are still young enough to enjoy your life.
   Before you are too old to lead an active life.
7. Someone who is honest enough to be trusted with the responsibility.
   Someone who is too honest to listen to rich fund-raisers.
8. He or she should be tall enough to reach the basket easily.
   He or she should be able to run fast enough to outdistance an opponent.
9. They aren't intelligent enough to do it.
   Their brains are too underdeveloped.

Exercise 7

1. The world's forests are being destroyed at such an alarming rate that we can't ignore the problem any longer.
2. The world population is growing so quickly that we can't continue our old habits.
3. We have so few alternative materials that we haven't stopped using trees for fuel.
4. There has been such a rapid growth in population that there are no other places for people to live except the rain forests.
5. Some countries have so few other natural resources that they are forced to exploit the rain forests for economic development.
6. The problems appear so insurmountable that some countries haven't even begun to address them.
7. The United Nations considers deforestation such a problem that they are trying to establish conservation programs throughout the developing world.
8. The loss of the rain forests is such a major global threat that the future of mankind may be at stake.

Exercise 8

1. Plant species are being wiped out so quickly that we won't be able to find out if they have important medical uses.
2. We know so little about the relationship between rain forests and weather patterns that we can't take a chance.
3. So little is known about the various medical uses of plants in the rain forests that we must not risk destroying them.
4. So many people are hoping to become rich from cutting down the rain forests that we can't expect much change in the situation.
5. Some people fear that others are so greedy that they will never consider the long-term effects on the planet.

Exercise 9

(1) they become funny   (4) everyone ends up laughing   (6) everything froze   (10) dogs and cats froze when they went outside; birds fell out of the sky, frozen solid   (12) people's words froze whenever they tried to talk   (17) nobody could carry on a conversation because the words just froze right up; to wear shorts   (18) everything became unfrozen all at the exact same minute   (19) everyone became deaf

Exercise 10

Answers will vary. Possible answers include:

1. I'm such a good student that I always do my homework before class.
   I'm so lazy that I never do my homework.
2. I drive so quickly that I get a speeding ticket once a week.
   I'm such a slow walker that it takes me a week to get to grammar class.
3. I once wanted a new bicycle so badly that I saved every penny of my allowance for over a year.
   I wanted to visit Brazil so much that I read everything I could find about it.
4. I once ate so much food that I got sick.
   I once ate so much ice cream that I couldn't stand to eat any more for over a year.
5. They're so high that the tops of the mountains are permanently covered with snow.
   They're so high that climbers have to carry oxygen with them when they climb them.
6. I was so young, I can't remember.
   My memory is so bad, I can't even remember what I did yesterday.
7. He was so tall that he had to duck every time he went through a doorway.
   He was so tall that he had to buy his clothing at a special store.
8. It's so hard, that many people have to take it several times before they get a good score.
   It's so hard that some people try to cheat when they take it.
9. It was so boring that even the teacher fell asleep.
   It was so boring that nothing ever happened.
10. My grammar teacher is so wonderful that I'm going to name my first-born child after her.
    He is so wonderful that he can answer any question.

Activities

Activity 1

The interview process can be performed either in class or out of class. If possible, get students to compare responses of Americans versus international students or responses of young people versus old people.

Activity 2

Can be used as a brain-storming preparation activity for a writing assignment.

Activity 3

This should be a *fun* activity. All work and no play, etc., etc.

Activity 4

The sharing can be done in small groups, and the group can then choose one story to report to the rest of the class.

Activity 5

You may choose to omit the "problem solving" part of this task, but it is a useful opportunity to review and reinforce modals and patterns of giving advice.

Activity 6

A logical follow-up for Activity 1.

Activity 7

This can also be a discussion topic for small groups or the whole class.

Factual, Inferential, and Predictive Conditionals

Task

Possible correct statements can be found in Exercise 3.

Exercise 1

This is an open-ended exercise.

1. (3) **(condition)** if someone had a physical deformity; **(result)** they usually ended up working in a circus   (5) **(condition)** Whenever the circus came to town; **(result)** people would stand in long lines and pay large amounts of money for the opportunity to see Chang and Eng   (9) **(condition)** If Chang drank whiskey; **(result)** Eng got drunk   (10) **(condition)** Whenever Eng felt hungry; **(result)** Chang (who spoke better English) had to ask for food   (11) **(condition)** If they got into an argument about something; **(result)** they would sometimes spend days not speaking to each other

2. (2) **(condition)** If the climate continues to grow warmer; **(result)** the polar ice caps will begin to melt and the level of the world's oceans will rise   (3) **(result)** Weather patterns will be affected, and areas of the planet that now get a lot of rain will get considerably less   (6) **(condition)** If the world community can slow the wide-scale destruction of the world's rain forests; **(result)** this might also slow down the process a little bit   (9) **(condition)** If these droughts continue for another year; **(result)** there will not be enough water to support the present populations in those areas, and it will be necessary to ration water, or perhaps to sell it like gasoline, a liter at a time

Exercise 2

If there is milk, I have cold cereal for breakfast.

If I have forgotten to buy milk, I usually have toast.

If I have an early meeting, I leave at 6:00.

If it's a normal day, I leave at 7:00.

If I drive to work, it usually takes about 45 minutes.

If I take the bus, it usually takes an hour and a half.

If there is a traffic jam on the freeway, it can take an hour or even an hour and a half.

If traffic continues to get worse, I don't know what I'll do.

If current trends continue, it will soon take four hours a day to get to and from work.

Exercise 3

1. factual
2. inferential
3. factual
4. factual
5. inferential
6. predictive
7. factual
8. predictive
9. factual
10. predictive

Exercise 4

Answers will vary. Possible paraphrases include:

1. Children will grow up to be rude if they aren't disciplined.

   If you don't spank children when they are naughty, they will end up being brats.

2. You shouldn't criticize someone if you have the same problem yourself.

   You shouldn't say bad things about someone if you have any shortcomings yourself.

3. If you repair something right away, you will save yourself lots of time in the long run.

   If you postpone fixing a problem while it is small, it may get bigger and bigger, and be very difficult to fix.

4. If you can't do anything about a problem, there's no point in complaining about it.

   Don't be upset about something that has already happened.

5. If you get married before you know a person well, you may regret it later.

   If you don't think carefully about what you're going to do, you may end up making a big mistake.

6. If someone works all the time, they will have a boring life.

   If you don't take time to rest and relax, you can't think clearly or perform your job well.

Exercise 5

Answers will vary. Possible answers include:

1. *When you were a child, what would happen if you got bad grades in school?*

   If I got bad grades in school, my parents never let me watch TV.

   …my parents made sure I did my homework every night.

2. *When you were a child, what would happen if you told a lie?*

   If I told a lie, my parents sometimes spanked me.

   …my parents usually found out the truth from my brother.

3. *When you were a child, what would happen if you hit your brother or sister?*

   If I hit my brother or sister, they usually hit me back.

   …my parents usually spanked me.

4. *When you were a child, what would happen if you got good grades in school?*

   If I got good grades in school, my parents always gave me a lot of praise.

   …my parents sometimes gave me a special gift.

5. *When you were a child, what would happen if you helped with chores?*

   If I helped with chores, my parents usually paid me an allowance.

   …nothing special happened, but if I didn't help, my parents sometimes got angry.

6. *When you were a child, what would happen if you fell down and hurt yourself?*

   If I fell down and hurt myself, my mother always kissed me and made me feel better.

   …I usually cried.

7. *When you were a child, what would happen if you disobeyed your parents?*
   If I disobeyed my parents, I usually got punished.
      ...I sometimes felt guilty.
8. *When you were a child, what would happen if you did not want to go to bed?*
   If I did not want to go to bed, I usually asked my father to tell me a story.
      ...I often asked my parents to let me stay up later.

Exercise 6

Answers will vary. Possible answers include:

- **In the United States, if a teacher...**
  - sits on a desk, students will think he is relaxed.
  - wears blue jeans to school, students will think he's "cool."
  - says "I don't know," students will respect her for her honesty.
  - makes a lot of jokes in class, students will probably enjoy it.
  - hits a student, she might be fired from her job.
  - makes a mistake, he will probably admit that he was wrong.
  - doesn't give the students homework, they will probably think the teacher isn't doing a very good job.

- **In the United States, if a student...**
  - comes late to class, the teacher may be insulted.
  - doesn't understand the lesson, he is expected to ask the teacher for extra help.
  - asks a question, the teacher will think the student is paying attention and is interested in the lesson.
  - makes jokes in class, the teacher might think the student isn't serious.
  - doesn't do the homework, the teacher will probably give him a bad grade.
  - copies another student's answers, the teacher will punish the student.
  - makes a mistake, the teacher usually isn't concerned, because she knows that the student is trying his best.

Exercise 7

1. predictive
2. inferential
3. inferential
4. predictive
5. predictive
6. predictive
7. inferential
8. predictive

Exercise 8

Answers will vary. Possible answers include:

1. if you study hard; if you keep trying.
2. if we reduce our use of fossil fuels; if the government develops new sources of energy.
3. if I don't do my best work; if Bambang doesn't come late.

4. if people don't try to get along; if we keep selling arms to developing countries.
5. if we don't start improving public transportation; if new roads are built.
6. if the landlord raises our rent; if we can't renew our lease.
7. if we don't reduce our use of fossil fuels; if the government doesn't develop new sources of energy.
8. if I don't get good grades; if I can't find a job.
9. if I pass the TOEFL; if she gives me an *A* in this class; if hell freezes over.
10. if they continue to get cheaper and easier to use; if we don't have a new period like the Dark Ages.

Exercise 9

Answers will vary. Possible answers include:

1. I might get an *A* in this class; I might pass the TOEFL.
2. the oceans could rise; weather patterns could change.
3. I may start taking the bus to work; air pollution may get worse too.
4. I will tell them I love them and miss them; I will ask for money.
5. I won't get admitted to the university; I won't be able to go home for vacation.
6. I will be very sad; I will have to spend another semester studying English.
7. I won't have to take it again next semester; I won't need to take the TOEFL.
8. my teacher will be angry with me; I will have a hard time understanding today's lesson.

Exercise 10

Answers will vary. Possible answers include:

1. *If my partner is called to serve in the army,...*
   he will probably flee the country; he will try to enlist in the air force.
2. *If my partner gets the flu,...*
   she usually takes lots of vitamin C; she stays home in bed until she feels better.
3. *If my partner needs money for school,...*
   his parents usually send it to him; he will look for a part-time job.
4. *If my partner wins the lottery,...*
   she will be very happy; she'll buy a new car.
5. *If my partner falls in love with an American,...*
   her parents might be disappointed; he might get married.
6. *If my partner gets lost in a strange city,...*
   she usually asks someone for directions; she tried to find her location on a map.
7. *If my partner sees someone committing a crime,...*
   she will call the police; she will try to remember what the criminal looks like.
8. *If my partner starts getting homesick,...*
   he usually calls his family; she will try to keep busy.

Exercise 11

Answers will vary. Possible answers include:

1. Then I guess we'd better study tonight.   Then maybe you shouldn't cut class.
2. Then you should stop eating sweets.   Then you ought to do some exercise every day.
3. Then let's open a window.   Then why don't you take off that wool sweater.
4. Then let's go shopping this weekend.   Then you'd better see if you have enough money to buy some.
5. Then let's go to the movies.   Then why don't you call up some friends and make a plan?
6. Then you had better get medical insurance.   Then don't get sick!
7. Then you should ask Mary if you can look at her notes.   Then you didn't hear that we are going to have a test next week.

Exercise 12

Answers will vary. Possible answers include:

1. If so, we had better try to develop cleaner sources of energy.   If so, we need to be prepared for the changes.

    If not, smog is still a health problem.   If not, there must be some explanation for the continuing drought in Africa.

2. If so, it seems like a good idea to use one whenever you're in a car.   If so, it makes a lot of sense to require people to wear them.

    If not, avoiding accidents is the best way to keep from getting injured.   If not, it's not important to buckle up.

3. If so, there's a good reason to restrict smoking in public places.   If so, people shouldn't be allowed to smoke in offices, stores, theaters, or restaurants.

    If not, people might still object to smoking, because of the unpleasant smell.   If not, it wouldn't hurt for people to be a little more tolerant of other people's bad habits.

4. If so, colleges should have some flexibility in the score they require for admission.   If so, academic records should be more important for university admission than performance on TOEFL.

    If not, requiring a specific score seems like a good way to make sure that only good students will be accepted.   If not, it's crucial to get a good score when you are applying to school.

5. If so, it makes sense to reduce the amount of fat in your diet.   If so, we had better watch what we eat more carefully.

    If not, I think I'll start eating more red meat and butter.   If not, eating fatty foods still makes it difficult to lose weight.

Exercise 13

1. **not dependent:** Boiling water will eventually evaporate whether or not it is boiled rapidly.
2. **not dependent:** People must pay taxes in the United States whether or not they are American citizens.
3. **not dependent:** Students in American classrooms are expected to do homework whether or not they were absent from class the day before.
4. **dependent:** Marbles will roll to the outside edges of a plate if the plate is rotated rapidly.
5. **dependent:** Two objects will fall at the same rate of speed if they have the same weight.
6. **dependent:** Two objects will fall at the same rate of speed if they have the same mass.
7. **dependent:** Most universities will admit foreign students if they get a high score on the TOEFL.
8. **not dependent:** Automobile accidents may occur whether or not the driver is wearing a seat belt.
9. **dependent:** Injuries may be less serious if the driver is wearing a seat belt.
10. **dependent:** The rate of global warming will decrease if worldwide emissions of CO_2 are decreased.

Exercise 14

Answers will vary. Possible answers include:

1. unless you study harder; unless you take it more than once.
2. unless we do something about it; unless there is a change in how we use fossil fuels.
3. unless we stop selling arms to developing countries; unless the United Nations takes a more powerful role in world affairs.
4. unless we improve public transportation; unless people start to carpool whenever possible.
5. unless he starts to work harder; unless Mr. Green agrees to give him a raise.
6. unless we start to develop solar energy; unless we start to conserve the resources we have now.
7. unless my parents send me money for tuition; unless I can get permission to work part-time to meet expenses.
8. unless scientists discover an effective vaccine or treatment; unless the government spends more money on education and prevention.

Activities

Activity 1

This activity offers an opportunity to discuss some of the cross-cultural differences in teacher and student behaviors. Giving the students a clear explicit understanding of what is expected of teachers and students in your classroom is probably even more important than correct use of conditional structures.

Activities 2 and 3

These give students a chance to use predictive conditionals. They can be used as testing or diagnostic activities by having the students write their responses.

Activity 4

An open-ended version of Exercise 2.

Activity 5

Unit 18, Exercise 2 contains a text illustrating the law of supply and demand.

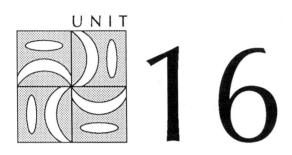

UNIT 16 — Adverbials of Purpose and Reason

Task

This task can also be used earlier in the course to help students identify some of their reasons and purposes for studying English. This is an important first step in getting students to formulate learning goals.

Exercise 1

1. reason
2. reason
3. purpose
4. reason
5. purpose
6. reason
7. reason

Exercise 2

This is an open-ended exercise.

(2) **(R)** because they enjoy being physically active; **(P)** because they want to control their weight, or have a more muscular physique or improve their cardiovascular fitness   (4) **(P)** for a particular purpose   (5) **(R)** because they enjoy the activity itself   (7) **(R)** because they enjoy the experience; **(P)** to obtain a particular benefit   (8) **(R)** if the benefit is too hard to achieve   (9) **(R)** because they were able to develop new eating habits and to enjoy those new habits   (10) **(P)** only to improve their physical appearance; **(R)** because they no longer have the extrinsic motivation to eat less, and they have not developed the intrinsic motivation to eat more sensibly

Exercise 3

Answers will vary. Possible answers include:

1. Because they are addicted to nicotine; Because they like the flavor.
   In order to appear more sophisticated; To "reward themselves" in some way.
2. Because they don't have opportunity at home; Because they are trying to escape political persecution.
   To experience living in a different culture; To get a chance for a better life.
3. Because they are curious about movie stars; Because they want to compare their lives with those of famous people.
   In order to have someone to gossip about; In order to feel better about their own lives.
4. Because certain illnesses are caused by poor diet; Because gaining weight is bad for health.
   In order to get adequate nutrition; In order to maintain a healthy body.
5. Because teachers expect you to; Because using a language is more important than knowing about a language.
   In order to practice what they have learned in class; In order to be prepared to express yourself in out-of-class situations.

6. Because they aren't bright enough to be scholars; Because they love power.

    In order to influence public policy; In order be in a position to tell other people what to do.

7. Because they want a way to assess language proficiency; Because the test is relatively reliable and easy to register for.

    To tell if students have the language ability to understand university-level work; To make sure that students have a good knowledge of listening, grammar, vocabulary, and reading.

8. Because they want to have children; Because their parents expect them to.

    In order to begin a family; To spend their lives with someone they love.

Exercise 4

Infinitives of purpose have been circled.

(1) John was anxious <u>to find</u> a French family who he could live with. (2) He wanted <u>to stay</u> with a family (to improve his conversational ability.) (3) He was about <u>to give up</u> looking when he saw a notice on the bulletin board at school. (4) He called right away (to make sure that the family was still looking for someone.) (5) He was delighted <u>to hear</u> that they were, and he made an appointment <u>to meet</u> them that very afternoon. (6) The family appeared <u>to be</u> friendly, so John decided <u>to move in</u> the following week. (7) He started eating meals with the family right away (to get) an opportunity <u>to practice</u> what he was learning in his classes, and (to start) getting <u>to know</u> them as quickly as possible.

Exercise 5

This is an open-ended exercise. Explanations may vary.

1. This is not an adverbial of purpose, but reason. The strange order emphasizes the importance of the nail.
2. The adverbial comes first in order to establish the purpose for the things that it is necessary to do.
3. Putting "for a great vacation" before the final clause helps emphasize the contrast between a good place (Hawaii) and a great place (Disneyland).
4. Emphasizes the reason. The order of reason/result is maintained.
5. Emphasizes the reason. The order of reason/result is maintained.
6. Emphasizes the reason. The order of reason/result is maintained.

Activities

Activities 1–3

Can be used as testing or diagnostic activities.

Activity 4

You may wish to eliminate the discussion questions at the end of the activity and just teach the song for its own sake or for the fun of it.

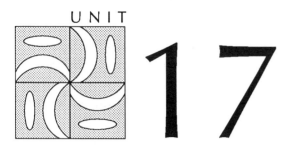

Relative Clauses

Additional Grammar Note:

> This unit does not discuss restrictive and nonrestrictive modification, except tangentially in Focus 2. This topic is treated in more detail in Book 4 of this series.

Task

Answers to the Think and Write section will vary. Some possible answers are listed below. They can be used as a diagnostic by evaluating the sentences generated in this part of the Task.

Which twin has children that are all girls?
  The twin who is married to Bernice has children that are all girls.
  The twin who has an old-fashioned bungalow-style home has children that are all girls.

Which twin owns a dog named Prince?
  The twin who likes to play football owns a dog named Prince.
  The twin who is married to a woman named Betty owns a dog named Prince.

Which twin told his children that he had been adopted?
  The twin who sells advertising space in magazines.

Which twin drinks Miller?
  The twin who likes to play football.

Which twin prefers basketball?
  The twin who drinks Budweiser.

Which twin lives in a ranch-style home?
  The twin who sells plumbing supplies.

Exercise 1

Answers may vary. Different logical connectors may be used, or even omitted from correct answers.

1. Jeff likes to get up early most days. On weekends, however, he prefers to sleep late.
2. Denise has too much work to do. As a result, she can't even consider taking a vacation.
3. Many people feel war is extremely destructive. As a result, they are opposed to military solutions for international problems.

4. I once met a man. He looked just like a friend of mine.
5. Bob is looking for a part-time job. He needs some extra money.
6. On some Saturday mornings, I clean the house. On other Saturday mornings, I go shopping.
7. I know an old lady. She swallowed a fly.
8. I have many friends. However, I still enjoy getting to know new people.

Exercise 2

The antecedents of the relative clauses have been circled. (N.B.: Sentence 9 contains a noun clause rather than a relative clause.)

(2) (the woman) that he has been looking for all his life   (3) (women) that are intelligent and independent, who have a good sense of humor and a love of adventure   (4) (The woman) that he has fallen in love with   (5) (the most important characteristic) that Charley is looking for   (6) (several other interests) that Charley also shares   (7) (the women) that he used to go out with   (8) (something) that he wasn't satisfied with   (10) (The "perfect woman") that he was looking for   (11) (the picture) that someone has in his or her imagination   (12) (someone) that he thinks is perfect

Exercise 3

(1) I finally met the woman **whom** Charley has fallen in love with. (2) She seems to be the kind of person **who** likes being active and adventurous. (3) She has a responsible position in a company **which** produces computer programs. (4) That's a field Charley is also interested in. (5) She likes hobbies **which** involve athletics and being outdoors. (6) She seems to like all of Charley's friends **whom** she has met so far, including me. (7) Maybe one of these days, I'll meet a woman **who's** like Charley's new girlfriend. (8) In the meantime, Charley had better hope that she doesn't meet a man **who's** like me! I just might try to ask her out myself!

Exercise 4

You may also wish to have students restate the relative clauses as independent sentences. Students should read the whole passage before doing the exercise.

EXAMPLES: I read (a book) **that** was published last year.
The book was published last year.

I read (a book) **which** your professor wrote.
Your professor wrote the book.

I met (the person) **whom** Charley gave flowers.
Charley gave flowers to the person.

I met (the person) **who** Charley told me about.
Charley told me about the person.

(1) I read (an article) the other day that interested me a great deal. (2) It reported on (a survey) that some sociologists conducted recently. (3) They examined (the attitudes) that American women have about men, and they identified some of (the things) that women consider to be important characteristics in a good husband or boyfriend. (4) The study determined that women seem prefer (men) who can express their feelings. (5) Most women prefer (husbands) who they can talk to easily, and who they can share their problems with. (6) There were also (several other things) that women consider important in a partner. (7) A man's character or personality is more important to many women than (the type of job) that he has, or (the amount of money) that he makes. (8) Not surprisingly, most women want (a husband) that will take on an equal share of housekeeping and child-raising duties. (9) But the bottom line is this: Women want (husbands) who they can trust and depend on. (10) Unfortunately, more than 70% of the women who answered the questionnaires said they had (husbands) who didn't meet these basic requirements in some way.

Exercise 5

The relative pronouns that can be deleted are listed below. Students should read the whole passage before doing the exercise.

(1) that; who are   (3) who are   (4) that are   (7) who are   (9) who are; that; that; that   (10) who are

Exercise 6

Students should read the whole passage before doing the exercise.

(2) the world had fought up to that time   (3) sent to battle from both sides   (4) the world had never before seen   (5) that had been previously impossible   (6) called mustard gas; which permanently damaged the lungs of soldiers; caught without gas-masks   (8) killed in action   (9) caused by the unsanitary conditions on the battlefield; which developed in lungs; damaged by mustard gas   (10) established by "the war to end all wars"   (11) the world had ever known; facing European governments at that time   (12) the winners had forced the losers to accept

Exercise 7

1. Charley has fallen in love with the woman to whom his cousin introduced him.
2. I no longer have a friend with whom I can go to the movies, now that Charley is spending all his free time with his new girlfriend.

3. World War I did not really provide a solution to the problems for which it was fought in the first place.
4. Turkey was one of the countries with which Germany was allied during World War I.
5. This is the article about which I told you.
6. Women prefer husbands with whom they can discuss their troubles and concerns.
7. Some of the issues about which my friends are concerned are environmental destruction, political activism, and developing alternative energy sources.

Exercise 8

1. Last month Charley fell in love with a young woman he had been introduced to by some mutual friends.
2. She had a number of positive characteristics Charley found quite attractive.
3. She was careful to leave time for other activities and interests that helped keep her healthy, and reflected her commitment to the needs of her friends and family.
4. She had a wonderful sense of humor, which made their times together relaxing and enjoyable.
5. From the first time they met, Charley felt there was a "special understanding" between them he was unable to explain.

Exercise 9

1. Bernice is married to a twin. The twin's dog is named King.
2. The twin's children are all girls. He told them about his background.
3. The children are all boys. Their father didn't tell them that he had been adopted.
4. Betty is married to a twin. The twin's dog is named Prince.
5. The modern ranch-style home belongs to a twin. His favorite sport is football.
6. Bernice is the wife of a twin. The twin's friends first reported that they had seen his "double."
7. Twins' upbringings are different. However, they still tend to have many characteristics in common.
8. People can have identical physical characteristics. They also tend to have similar personalities and interests.

Exercise 10

1. Florence met a man whose twin brother is a well-known geneticist.
2. Jeff and Matt, whose nickname is "Akbar," are roommates.
3. People whose genetic makeups are similar may have similar personalities.
4. Joan took a class from a teacher whose wife she knew in college.
5. Mary Rae would like to go to the lecture by the mountain climber whose latest climb she read about in *Adventure Magazine*.
6. My friend has a dog whose eyes are different colors.
7. I keep getting phone calls for some stranger whose last name is apparently the same as mine.
8. Charley finally succeeded in meeting the artist whose work he had been admiring for years.

Exercise 11

Answers will vary.

1. My brother bought a used car the tires of which need to be replaced immediately. *(very formal)* My brother bought a used car whose tires need to be replaced immediately. *(informal — but a little illogical, since the car is not a person.)*

   Possible restatements: The tires of the used car my brother bought need to be replaced immediately.   My brother bought a used car, but he needs to replace the tires immediately.

2. We'll be going to an opera the synopsis of which can be found in the program. *(very formal)* We'll be going to an opera whose synopsis can be found in the program. *(very formal — but a little illogical, since the opera is not a person.)*

   Possible restatements: You can find the synopsis of the opera we'll be going to in the program.   We'll be going to an opera, and you can find a synopsis in the program.

3. I saw a mysterious-looking symbol, the meaning of which was as mysterious as its design. *(very formal)* I saw a mysterious-looking symbol whose meaning was as mysterious as its design. *(informal — but a little illogical, since the symbol is not a person.)*

   Possible restatements: I saw a mysterious-looking symbol.   Its meaning was as mysterious as its design.

4. Darryl has finished his latest book the cover of which had his picture on it. *(very formal)* Darryl has finished his latest book whose cover had his picture on it. *(informal but somewhat illogical)*

   Possible restatements: Darryl has finished his latest book, and his picture is on the cover.   Darryl's picture is on the cover of his latest book, which he has just finished.

Exercise 12

1. My father can remember the old days when there were no televisions or computers.
2. I'm going to start reading again where I stopped reading last night.
3. Jeff grew up in a small town in Kansas where everybody knew everybody else.
4. Most people think New Orleans is a great place where everyone can live as they please.
5. Do you remember that Halloween party at Alice's house when everyone ran outside in their costumes and surprised the neighbors?

Exercise 13

(1) The Sixties were a time of rapid social change when many people explored alternative life-styles. (2) The change was greatest in urban areas where there were a lot of young people studying at universities and colleges. (3) San Francisco was one center of the hippie movement where many people gathered during the famous "Summer of Love" in 1967. (4) The Haight-Ashbury was the center of activity where people from all parts of the city came to listen to rock and roll concerts. (5) People today look back upon the Sixties as an important time when old values were brought into question, and people experimented with new answers.

Exercise 14

(1) We stayed at a hotel in Mexico where they had trained monkeys in the lobby. (2) We arrived at the hotel during a festival when all the hotels in town were full. (3) Someone had put our reservation in the wrong file where no one else could find it. (4) They put us in a very small room where there were no windows. (5) Our vacation became much more pleasant on the next day when we were moved to a larger room.

Exercise 15

(1) Charley wants to make some changes in his life which/that involve both his life-style and his social activities. (2) Charley wants to find a new place to live where there is enough room for a dog. (3) He plans to move next year when the lease on his old apartment expires. (4) He's looking at a new apartment where there is a balcony, so he can grow some flowers. (5) Charley also wants to get married to someone whose political beliefs are similar to his own. (6) He hasn't found anyone yet who seems to share his interest in politics and sports. (7) He often goes to coffee shops where people of similar interests go on weekends. (8) He's thinking of putting a personals ad in a paper where a lot of people advertise in order to meet others with similar interests and backgrounds.

Activities

Activity 1

This activity is extremely popular with students, and always generates lively and spirited discussion. Teachers who have particularly strong views on this subject, or who feel they don't know how to handle student comments with which they personally disagree, are advised to choose a more innocuous activity.

Activity 2

You may wish to follow the procedure for the Task in Unit 13 for correcting the errors in students' essays.

Activity 3

A good activity for a late Friday afternoon class.

Activity 4

See comments for Activity 1.

Activity 6

Such introductions are often written ahead of time, even by native speakers.

Activities 7 and 8

These work best as "discussion" topics.

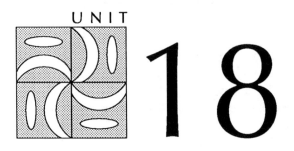

Unit 18

Special Problems in Using Present Time

Temporary versus Permanent, Actions versus States

Task

Examples of the kinds of sentences students should write have been provided in the Task. This can easily be used for testing or diagnosis by having the students turn in their paragraphs, rather than comparing them with another student's.

Exercise 1

EXPERIMENT 1:

(1) When baking soda **is** added to vinegar, a chemical reaction **occurs**. (2) The baking soda **bubbles** and CO_2 **is** produced by the combination of elements. (3) When a candle **is** put next to the container while the chemical reaction **is** taking place, the flame on the candle **will go (goes)** out.

EXPERIMENT 2:

(4) We **want** to determine whether gravity **affects** the rate of acceleration of objects falling through space. (5) Two objects of similar size and shape, but substantially different weights — a cannonball and a volleyball — **are** dropped from the same height. (6) We **find** that both objects **hit** the ground at the same time. (7) This **indicates** that the attraction of gravity **is** constant.

Exercise 2

(1) In rural areas, before the development of **(without)** good interregional transportation, the price of **commodities is** determined by the relationship between its supply and the demand for it. (2) Supply **is** determined by how much **of the commodity is** available. (3) Demand **is** determined by how many people **need** to buy it. (4) When the demand for **a particular commodity rises,** the price also **rises.** (5) **Producers respond** to the price increase by producing more of **the commodity,** since they **can** get a more profitable return on their investment of time and effort because of the higher prices. (6) With more of the **commodity** available, the competition to sell **it** also **increases,** and the prices of the **commodity begin** to drop. (7) Fluctuations in **commodity** prices **are** extreme and continuous.

(8) But with the development of better interregional transportation, a more constant supply **becomes** available, since extra **commodities can** be brought in from other places. (9) Similarly, a more constant demand **exists,** since **commodities can** be sent to other areas of the country where harvests **have** not been as good.

Exercise 3

1. am talking
2. speaks
3. is studying
4. leave
5. is making (this time)/makes (every time)
6. is doing (this time)/does (every time)
7. am trying
8. are discovering
9. is getting/gets
10. gets

Exercise 4

(1) isn't taking   (2) doesn't think   (3) has   (4) teaches/is teaching   (5) gets   (6) don't make   (7) is looking for   (8) is trying   (9) hire   (10) is finding   (11) is getting   (12) searches   (13) is beginning   (14) wants

Exercise 5

Answers will vary. Possible answers include:

I wake up at 7:00. I have breakfast and read the paper. I take a shower and get dressed. I drive to work. It usually takes about an hour. I usually exercise during my lunch hour, and I leave the office around 4:30 or 5:00. I watch the TV news when I get home, then I make myself dinner. I usually go to bed around 10:30 or 11:00 and read for a while before I fall asleep.

I'm not eating breakfast these days, because I'm trying to lose weight.

I'm not driving to work because my car is being repaired.

I'm not exercising at lunch because my coworkers are workaholics and schedule meetings for every available moment of the day.

Exercise 6

Answers will vary. Possible answers include:

1. What kind of fruit tastes best with ice cream?

   Fruits that aren't too sweet taste best with ice cream.

2. What way do you think is most effective to learn a foreign language?

   The most effective way to learn a foreign language is to use it whenever possible.

3. How does a sick person often appear?

   He might appear flushed or feverish. Sometimes he might just appear tired.

4. What does your notebook contain?

   It contains all the things I'm supposed to do. I have trouble remembering my appointments, so I have to write them down.

5. What does a handshake mean in your culture?

   It means that two people have reached an agreement about something. It's like an unwritten contract.

6. What activity do your parents appreciate your doing?

   They appreciate my studying hard.

7. What does getting a BA degree require?

   It usually requires finishing at least 120 units of course-work.

8. How many neckties do you own?

   I only own five, but that's because I don't wear a coat and tie to work.

9. Who does that Mercedes belong to?

   I know it doesn't belong to our grammar teacher. English teachers never get paid enough.

10. What don't you understand about American Culture?

    I don't understand how people become close friends in this country.

Exercise 7

Answers will vary. See Exercise 6 for possible examples.

Exercise 8

1. feels
2. am considering
3. are being/are
4. believe; is having
5. tastes
6. mind
7. doubts
8. looks/is looking
9. feels/is feeling
10. requires
11. is requiring/requires
12. are being/are

Exercise 9

There I **am**, standing in dirty swamp water as deep as my waist, but **I'm** having a wonderful time! The canoe **we're rowing has** gotten stuck on a log, so somebody **has** to get into the water and try to lift one end of it. I **look** into the water. It **looks** really dark and dirty. I **know** there **are** a lot of poisonous snakes in this area. I **know** there **are** also alligators. All of a sudden, I **realize** that **I'm** not afraid of any of these things. I **have** complete confidence in my ability to free the canoe and to avoid getting eaten or bitten. Without another thought, I **jump** into the water and **start** to pull at the canoe. At that moment, I **know** that there **is** nothing that **I'm** afraid to do, and nothing that I **can't** do if I put my mind to it. Outward Bound **is** one of the most important experiences of my life!

Activities

There are a variety of activities in this unit. **Activity 1** adapts well to a "how-to" speech assignment. **Activities 2** and **4** can be used as diagnostic or testing activities. **Activities 3** and **5** can be done as written activities or as cross-cultural discussion topics in small groups or with the class as a whole.

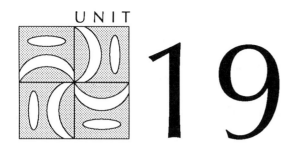

UNIT 19

Special Problems with Present Perfect Tense

Describing Past Events in Relation to the Present

Task

See **"Teaching a Sample Unit"** for a complete discussion of how to teach the Task, Exercises, and Activities of this Unit.

Exercise 1

(1) *(a)* — makes; *(a)* — is   (2) *(a)* — am   (3) *(a)* — is; *(b)* — have had   (4) *(b)* — has given   (5) *(c)* — was   (6) *(c)* — taught   (7) *(c)* — was   (8) *(c)* — was; *(c)* — was   (9) *(b)* — have lived; *(b)* — have lived; *(b)* — has been   (10) *(b)* — have always been able to be   (11) *(b)* — have learned; *(a)* — are; *(a)* — have   (12) *(b)* — have learned   (13) *(b)* — have learned; *(a)* — doesn't necessarily mean   (14) *(b)* — has made; *(b)* — has helped

Exercise 2

(1) came   (2) has been   (3) has had   (4) cooked   (5) has had   (6) required   (7) has found   (8) was   (9) has not quite adjusted   (10) has learned   (11) has been   (12) had   (13) has met   (14) was   (15) planned   (16) has changed   (17) got/has gotten   (18) has spoken/spoke   (19) hasn't decided

Exercise 3

Answers will vary. Possible answers include:

1. *Have you ever…(ridden a horse, been in love, seen a flying saucer…)?*
   Yes, I have.   No I haven't.
2. *How many times have you…(eaten Chinese food, taken the TOEFL, driven a motorcycle…)?*
   I've done it many times.   I've only done it once or twice.   I've done it often, but I've never inhaled.
3. *Name three things you have never done but would like to do.*
   I've never been to the Seychelles, but I'd like to go.   I've never become a movie star…   I've never fallen in love…
4. *Name three things you have done that you don't particularly want to do again.*
   I've served on a jury.   I've been in love with someone who didn't love me.   I've written a grammar book.

SAMPLE REPORT OF STUDENT ANSWERS:

My partner has had an interesting life. She has visited seven foreign countries. She has flown an airplane. She hasn't been in a submarine, and she doesn't know how to swim. She hasn't begun her university study, but she is anxious to do so. She has taken the TOEFL several times and wishes that she didn't have to take it again.

Exercise 4

(1) just found out/has just found out (2) has won/won (3) has bought/bought (4) has never won/never won (5) won (6) has changed (7) has gotten (8) have been/were (9) won (10) has thought about

Exercise 5

1. (b) 2. (a) 3. (a) 4. (b) 5. (a)/(b) 6. (a)

Exercise 6

This is an open-ended activity. Possible explanations include:

1. There is a logical relationship to NOW. The passage connects past discoveries with the current fact that they are planning another space probe in the future.
2. There is an implied logical relationship. This suggests that the speaker has just been offered broccoli.
3. There is a chronological relationship with this moment. The listener is now hearing the news for the first time.
4. Like the first passage, previous information is relevant to the current situation.
5. This seems to be connected with NOW in the writer's mind. Perhaps the writer is going to make a new point about Shakespeare's understanding of psychology.
6. Connected with NOW in the speaker's mind. She has a job possibility for Jill at this moment.

Exercise 7

1. have been reading; have learned
2. has been crying
3. has resented
4. have been trying
5. have tried
6. have been working
7. has been expecting
8. has told
9. has been trying; have called
10. has dreamed/has been dreaming; has become

Exercise 8

PARAGRAPH 1

(1) speaks (2) learned/has learned (3) is studying/studies (4) is planning/plans (5) gets (6) has been living (7) is thinking (8) misses/is missing (9) is affecting/has affected/has been affecting (10) is considering/has considered (11) hasn't done so

PARAGRAPH 2

(1) have drawn/draws (2) have argued/argue (3) are (4) are (5) affect (6) encountered (7) was (8) have made (9) consider/have considered (10) feel (11) don't consist (12) has changed (13) deal (14) govern

Activities

Activity 1

This can be used as a testing activity. Students can refer to the essay in Exercise 1 for some ideas as to form.

Activity 2

This is an open-ended activity. The process of careful observation and hypothesis formation is the important part of the activity.

You may wish to bring in articles for the students to look at or let them choose articles on subjects of interest.

Activity 3

The first part of this activity can be used for diagnosis or testing by having students write their classmates responses as full sentences.

Have you changed any habits or routines recently?

Describe the changes.

Why have you made the changes?

How have the changes affected you?

Activities 4 and 5

These can be done as discussion activities in the context of cross-cultural differences.

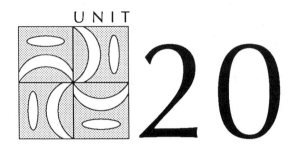

UNIT 20

Special Problems with Future Time

Using Present Tenses; Using *Will* versus *Going To*; Adverbial Clauses in Future Time

Task

The final paragraph called for in this exercise can be used to determine whether students are having trouble with these forms and whether additional practice with future time, prediction, or inference (Unit 21) is necessary.

Exercise 1

This is an open-ended exercise.

2. (1) *(a)* — 're having   (2) *(a)* — ends; *(a)* — will be; *(b)* — 're already making   (3) *(b)* — are being   (4) *(b)* — makes; *(a)* — 's bringing   (5) *(a)* — should be   (6) *(b)* — is being   (7) *(b)* — says; *(a)* — will come; *(b/c–refusal)* — won't bring   (8) *(c–request)* — Will you explain   (9) *(c–request)* — Will you tell; *(b)* — is   (10) *(b/c–obligation)* — should be   (11) *(a/b)* — is bringing   (12) *(b/c–refusal)* — won't

3. (1) *(a)* — should be   (2) *(b/c–advice)* — should be   (3) *(a)* — don't begin; *(a)* — could be   (4) *(b)* — is increasing   (5) *(b/c–refusal)* — will not put   (6) *(b)* — are decreasing; *(b/c–refusal)* — will not adequately support   (7) *(a)* — starts   (8) *(b)* — is; *(b)* — are or are not being taken; *(a)* — will determine; *(a)* — will be

Exercise 2

Answers will vary. Possible answers include:

What time do classes start next Tuesday?

When are we having our next grammar test?

When does the semester end?

Which unit do we study next?

When do we have to make our speeches?

When is the next TOEFL?

Exercise 3

1. (1) won't/isn't going to   (2) will/is going to   (3) will   (4) will
2. (1) will   (2) is going to/will   (3) is going to/will   (4) will
3. (1) will/am going to   (2) will/is going to   (3) will   (4) will
4. (1) is going to/will   (2) won't/isn't going to   (3) will   (4) will   (5) won't
5. (1) will   (2) will   (3) will   (4) will

Exercise 4

Answers will vary. Possible answers include:

1. Life should be better, because of all the technological advancements.

   Life might be worse, because the population is growing too rapidly.

2. There might be enough coal and oil, if we can start to conserve them now.

   There won't be enough coal and oil, because we haven't developed alternative energy sources.

3. There could be a decrease in air pollution if we stop using fossil fuels.

   There won't be a decrease in air pollution, because companies are unwilling to change their production techniques.

4. The overall climate may grow warmer, because we keep producing CO_2.

   The overall climate may not get warmer, because of continuing volcanic eruptions producing smoke and ash worldwide.

5. The rate of population growth will be greater, because the government is doing nothing about birth control.

   The rate of population growth might be lower, because it seems to drop when society becomes more industrialized.

6. There may be an increased use of automobiles if the government continues its lack of support for public transportation.

   There probably won't be an increased use of automobiles, because we are running out of petroleum.

7. There might be political stability if the world economy stabilizes.

   There probably won't be political stability because people never can get along with each other.

8. There will still be large differences between developing and developed countries because the international monetary system favors developed countries.

   There might not be large differences between developing and developed countries if a global economy continues to develop.

9. There will probably be cures for cancer and AIDS, but there will also probably be new diseases that mankind hasn't discovered yet.

10. People will probably face the same kind of problems in the twenty-first century.

    People won't have to worry about health or economic problems, because science will solve all the problems.

11. There will probably still be wars, because people don't seem to get along with each other.

    There won't be any more wars, because we will have a single global government.

Exercise 5

1. All my friends will be very relieved when the semester ends in a couple of weeks.
2. I'm going to go to the movies every day once I have finished all the household chores that have been postponed all semester.
3. It will be almost three weeks after the last day of class by the time Janet finally gets her research paper completed.
4. I'm going to read that book about magic when I have some time after the exams.
5. Peter's going to spend every afternoon at the beach while the weather is sunny.
6. Matt and Jeff will be really tired by the time they arrive in Phoenix by bicycle.
7. Kevin and Libby are leaving for Europe as soon as they finish their last exam.
8. Doug and Kathy are going to get married while they are on vacation in Mexico.
9. Even our teacher's going to take some time off when she has finished grading the final papers and correcting the exams.
10. The vacation will be over before we realize it/that sad news.

Exercise 6

This is an open-ended exercise. You may wish to omit this exercise if students have already studied Unit 2 and are not having trouble with the concepts taught there.

(1) *(a)* — will be   (2) *(moment of focus)* — the end of the twenty-first century; *(b)* — will have occurred   (3) *(a)* — are; *(b)* — will have been wiped out   (4) *(b)* — will have found   (5) *(c)* — will be living; *(b)* — are.   (6) *(d)* — will have been eating   (7) *(a)* — will, on the whole, be; *(b)* — are   (8) *(d)* — will have been researching   (9) *(b)* — is; *(a)* — will be   (10) *(b)* — will have removed   (11) *(d)* — will have been thinking; *(a)* — will no longer be

Activities

Activity 1

Having the students write their responses will give you a good opportunity to check their understanding and mastery of future time frame.

Activity 2

This can be a useful exercise to use before actual vacation periods. Sometimes students are lonely and bored during vacation times, and this activity can help them plan activities to keep busy.

Activity 3

This activity lends itself very well to a "formal debate" setting. You will need to help students organize the formalities (presentation, rebuttal, etc.) of the debate if they haven't already learned them in other classes.

UNIT 21

Modals of Prediction and Inference

Task

The focus of this Task lies in the distinction between making predictions versus logical deductions/inferences. The final explanations, based on the clues at the end of the chapter, should elicit *must*.

Exercise 1

Alternative choices have also been given.

1. Andy **should** decide what to do about his car next week.
2. The car **won't** work well enough for his trip to New York.
3. Andy **may/might** get it repaired, if it can be done cheaply.
4. He **shouldn't** have trouble selling it.
5. He **should** be able to get a good price.
6. Andy's friend Paul **might/may** want to buy it.
7. Andy **might/may** not sell the car to Paul.
8. The car **might/may** not be in very good condition.
9. The car **may/might** not be in very good condition.
10. Paul **could/might** expect a refund if he has troubles with the car.
11. Andy **will** need the money to buy a plane ticket if he doesn't drive.

Exercise 2

Answers will vary. All modals are possible in most situations, but likely answers include:

I won't be doing English homework.
I could/may/might/should be watching TV.
I (all modals are possible) thinking about personal problems.
I won't be going to church.
I may/might/could be reading a magazine.
I shouldn't/won't be taking a bath.
I could/might/be speaking another language.
I won't/shouldn't be sleeping.
I could/shouldn't writing letters to the family.
I will be having a good time with friends.

Exercise 3

Answers will vary. Possible answers include:

I will go someplace warm.   I will go someplace with a beach.
I should have a good time.   I should get a good tan.
I might go with friends.   I might travel there alone.
I might not go with friends.   I may not have enough money to fly there.
I shouldn't have much trouble meeting people.   I shouldn't plan on getting much work done.
I won't go anyplace cold.   I won't stay anyplace really expensive.

Exercise 4

Answers will vary. Possible answers include:

Life will be more complex.   There will be better communication.
Life should be more comfortable for most people.   Communication between countries should be easier.
Life may be better.   Life may be worse.
The standard of living might not be better.   Things may not have improved much compared to life today.
The world shouldn't be less complicated.   People's personal worries shouldn't be too different from the ones they have today.
I won't be alive.   My parents won't be alive.

Exercise 5

This is an open-ended exercise.

1. should; could/may/might; could/may/might
2. can't/couldn't; shouldn't; shouldn't; must
3. might/may not; should; should/must
4. must; could/may/might; could/may/might; can't/couldn't/shouldn't; must not/can't
5. must; can't/couldn't; should/could/may/might; could/may/might
6. must not; must
7. might/could/may; must not

Exercise 6

1. general truth
2. general truth
3. general truth
4. specific prediction
5. general truth
6. general truth
7. specific prediction
8. statement of ability
9. general truth
10. general truth

Exercise 7

1. reasonable expectation
2. reasonable expectation
3. negative implication
4. negative implication
5. reasonable expectation
6. negative implication

Exercise 8

1. is going to
2. ought to
3. shouldn't *(phrasal modal not possible)*
4. has to
5. must not *(phrasal modal not possible)*
6. isn't going to
7. is just going to
8. Should *(phrasal modal not possible)*
9. must not *(phrasal modal not possible)*
10. have got to

Exercise 9

There has been a slight change in sentence 1 to increase the naturalness of the text.

(1) might have gone   (2) should have had   (3) might have taken; had   (4) must have been   (5) must not have liked

Exercise 10

This is an open-ended exercise. You may also wish to have students compare their answers with those answers they chose in Exercise 5. Several of the passages are quite similar, but differ in time frame.

1. can't/couldn't/must not have been; could/might/may have been; must have been
2. should have had; should/could/might have been; should/could/might have paid; must have been
3. must have failed; could/may/might have been; couldn't/shouldn't have been
4. couldn't have disappeared; may/might/could have been; may/might/could have been; must have left
5. couldn't have been; could/may/might have been; could/may/might have been; must have been

Exercise 11

Answers will vary. Possible answers include:

1. She must be thinking about John. She could have gotten a letter from John telling her that he had fallen in love with a French girl.
2. He might be waiting for someone to arrive. His plane might have gotten delayed.
3. She must have done something that made them very proud of her. She could be graduating from college.
4. They might have been searching for treasure. They could have been planting trees.
5. She must have just won the lottery. She might have gotten a letter from her long-lost sister who had been kidnapped by Gypsies when they were babies at the convent.
6. He must be trying to get into an MBA program. He might be preparing for his graduate program.
7. He must be a homeless person. He must not have a family to take care of him. It must be America under the Republicans.
8. They must have gotten an alarm. There must have been a fire.

Activities

Activity 1

You may want the class to all watch the same program so that you can compare their interpretations with those of other students in the class. This can be used for testing or diagnosis by having the students write their descriptions. You will need to specify which time frame they should use in their description, or have them write the descriptions first in present and then in past time.

Activity 2

A simpler diagnostic activity than Activity 1.

Activity 3

The pictures show the following ingenious inventions

    Picture 1:   a candle snuffer

    Picture 2:   a hook to catch chickens

    Picture 3:   a cherry pit remover

    Picture 4:   a mechanical vegetable chopper

    Picture 5:   a glove dryer/stretcher

    Picture 6:   An ear protector for carriage horses

Activity 4

Students love this activity. You can poll the class to find out what other important additional signs and features of palm reading they are familiar with. It could be used as a diagnostic by having students write their predictions, but it might be more enjoyable just to relax and let the students have fun with this one.

UNIT 22

Hypothetical Statements

Additional Grammar Note:

> Hypothetical Meaning is a feature of English that causes the most difficulty for students from non-Indo-European language backgrounds. The forms of hypothetical speech are relatively straightforward, and students from languages such as French, Spanish, or even Persian have no difficulty understanding the basic concepts, although use varies considerably from language to language. Such students may be able to "breeze through" most of the exercises. However, speakers of Chinese, Indonesian, and many other languages do not have the same hypothetical notions expressed commonly in their own languages, and so therefore often find the meaning and use of hypothetical extremely difficult, even though they may have a relatively accurate understanding of the forms involved.
>
> Since hypothetical speech is extremely common in English, being used for strategies of politeness and indirectness and to indicate imaginary or hypothetical ideas, it is extremely important that students master the fundamental meaning and use dimensions as well as just the formal "conditionals contrary-to-fact" manipulations taught in most grammar texts.

Task

Students' understanding of hypothetical can be diagnosed by checking how their paragraphs or preparatory lists of their ideal lives would be different.

Exercise 1

1. a 2. a 3. b 4. b 5. a 6. b 7. a 8. a

Exercise 2

1. I was afraid of making mistakes.
2. I wasn't silly enough.
3. I took too many things seriously.
4. I didn't take enough trips.
5. I ate too many beans and not enough ice cream.
6. I didn't have many actual troubles, but I had a lot of imaginary ones.
7. I traveled too heavy.

8. I didn't start going barefoot until late in the spring.
9. I didn't go to enough dances.
10. I didn't ride enough merry-go-rounds.
11. I didn't pick enough daisies.

Exercise 3

1. I'm one of those people who lives sensibly and sanely hour after hour, day after day.
2. Oh, I've had my moments...
3. I've been one of those persons who never goes anywhere without a thermometer, a hot water bottle, a raincoat, and a parachute.

Exercise 4

1. hypothetical: I can't come to your party because I have to work.
2. prediction about a real event
3. hypothetical: Bill can't afford to retire, so he hasn't done so by now.
4. hypothetical: It's not a good idea to tease that dog!
5. hypothetical: I know you don't have your own jet, but let's imagine that we do. In our imaginations, where shall we go?... *(Notice that it's difficult to think of a way to restate this idea in nonhypothetical speech. That's how ingrained the pattern is in English.)*
6. prediction about a real event
7. prediction about a real event
8. prediction about a real event

Exercise 5

Match these statements with their correct implied meaning.

Statement **1(a)** matches implied meaning **1(b)**.
Statement **1(b)** matches implied meaning **1(a)**.
Statement **2(a)** matches implied meaning **2(b)**.
Statement **2(b)** matches implied meaning **2(a)**.
Statement **3(a)** matches implied meaning **3(b)**.
Statement **3(b)** matches implied meaning **3(a)**.

Exercise 6

There may be slight variation in the phrasing of the hypothetical ideas, but the basic meaning should be as follows:

1. If I had a million dollars, I could afford to buy you a new car.
2. If I spoke English perfectly, I wouldn't have to study grammar.
3. If doctors didn't have to spend so many years in medical school, medical care wouldn't be so expensive.
4. If my mother knew how I am living now, she would worry about me.
5. If I were President of my country, I would have a lot of influence on world events.

6. If I didn't have many good friends, my life would be dull and frustrating. (wouldn't be busy and rewarding)
7. If the TOEFL weren't a difficult examination, many people could pass it on the first try.
8. If there weren't so many irregular verbs in English, it would be an easier language to learn.
9. If there were enough places in universities in other countries, many students wouldn't come to the United States for university study.
10. If the weather reporter hadn't forecast heavy rains for the entire day tomorrow, we would have the picnic.

Exercise 7

Answers will vary. Possible answers include:

1. I would be happy; I would be nervous about my English.
2. I would balance the budget; I would reduce military spending.
3. she would worry about whether I was getting enough to eat; she would want me to study harder.
4. I would never give homework; I would give everybody an *A*.
5. I wouldn't be studying in this class; I would be happy.
6. I would bring everyone in my family a present; I would start packing today.
7. I would buy a new car every year; I wouldn't have to find a part-time job.
8. it would be a miracle; I would probably be as conservative as they are.

Exercise 8

Answers will vary. Possible answers include:

1. if I had all the money I needed; if my parents supported me.
2. if I had enough money; if they could all get visas.
3. if attendance weren't required; if we already knew English.
4. if it never rained; if we never went outdoors.
5. if I weren't interested in learning it; if it weren't important for my future.
6. if I weren't applying to American universities; if I didn't care about my score.
7. if we didn't have to study grammar; if everyone followed the golden rule.
8. if she promised to give me an *A*; if pigs could fly.

Exercise 9

Answers will vary. Exercises 6, 7, and 8 can also be done in pairs as structured conversation practice.

Exercise 10

1. If my parents had spoken English when I was a baby, I wouldn't have had to learn it in school.
2. If English hadn't become a language of international business after World War II, most developing countries wouldn't require students to study it in high school.
3. If modern English hadn't developed from several different languages — French, German, Latin, Dutch, and even Norwegian — the grammar and spelling rules would have been less irregular.
4. If England hadn't been invaded by France in 1066, many French words would not have replaced the traditional Anglo-Saxon ones.

Exercise 11

Answers will vary. Possible answers include:

1. I wouldn't have had to study it in high school; I would have passed the TOEFL years ago.
2. we might be required to study German or Japanese instead of English; the history of the twentieth century would have been very different.
3. the verb system would have been easier to learn; it would have been much more like German than it is.
4. it would have been developed somewhere else; companies like IBM would never have gotten so big.
5. I wouldn't have had to buy this book; I would never have gotten to like the Beatles.
6. I wouldn't be studying English; I would be a citizen.
7. we would all eat our lunch at MacSushi; we would probably be studying Japanese.
8. I wouldn't have come to America; I would probably do it without their permission.
9. life wouldn't be as convenient as it is; there wouldn't be such a great information explosion.
10. I wouldn't be in this class; I wouldn't be studying this book.

Exercise 12

Answers will vary. Possible answers include:

1. if I hadn't wanted you to be here; if I had known you had to study.
2. if I had passed the TOEFL; if it hadn't been required for my education.
3. if the language hadn't developed from so many different languages; if it had been invented by a computer.
4. if their writing systems had been easier to transmit electronically; if they hadn't become so inexpensive and easily available.
5. if I had been elected President; if the Republicans hadn't been in charge for the last 12 years.
6. if the telephone hadn't been invented; if communications satellites hadn't been put into orbit.
7. if the USSR hadn't collapsed; if their economies hadn't declined.
8. if scientists hadn't first developed penicillin; if there had been other effective disease-fighting drugs.
9. if TV hadn't been invented; if progress hadn't been made in most technological areas.
10. if I hadn't been called on by my teacher; if I had stayed home and not come to class.

Exercise 13

Answers will vary. Exercises 10 and 11 can be done in pairs as structured conversation practice.

Exercise 14

This exercise is intended for additional practice and review. It may be omitted if students are not having difficulty with form, meaning, or use of hypothetical conditionals.

Exercise 15

This is an open-ended exercise.

1. (2) If governments stopped spending so much on arms, more money would be available for economic development, education, and health care.

(4) If countries formed joint regional defense programs, one or two "superpowers" would be less likely to see themselves as responsible for maintaining global stability.

(5) if the size of military forces were reduced — or even eliminated — then that money would be available for nonmilitary purposes. (6) This would enable governments to give more support to social programs. (7) Better social programs would improve social conditions. (8) Improved social conditions worldwide would reduce the need for wars even more.

POSSIBLE NONHYPOTHETICAL PARAPHRASES:

(2) Governments spend too much on arms, so not enough money is available for economic development, education, and health care.

(4) Countries haven't formed joint regional defense programs, so one or two "superpowers" may be likely to see themselves as responsible for maintaining global stability.

(5) Pacifists point out that the size of military forces has not been reduced or eliminated and therefore that money is not available for nonmilitary purposes. (6) This keeps governments from giving more support to social programs. (7) Ineffective social programs make bad social conditions worse. (8) Poor social conditions worldwide contribute to the need for wars even more.

2. (3) if Sir Isaac Newton hadn't decided to take a nap under an apple tree, he wouldn't have been hit on the head by a falling apple. (5) If Sir Alexander Fleming hadn't left his sandwich sitting on a laboratory windowsill and forgotten about it, he wouldn't have discovered the mold that contains penicillin. (7) Had Christopher Columbus correctly calculated the actual size of the earth, he would never have tried to reach Asia by sailing west. (8) If that hadn't happened, the European discovery of the New World might have occurred in 1592, instead of 1492.

POSSIBLE NONHYPOTHETICAL PARAPHRASES:

(3) For example, Sir Isaac Newton decided to take a nap under an apple tree and was hit on the head by a falling apple. (5) Sir Alexander Fleming left his sandwich sitting on a windowsill and forgot about it. That was how he discovered the mold that contains penicillin. (7) Christopher Columbus incorrectly calculated the actual size of the earth, and therefore tried to reach Asia by sailing west. (8) Because that happened, the European discovery of the New World occurred in 1492, instead of 1592.

3. (2) But its use wouldn't have grown as rapidly as it has, had certain Asian writing systems been able to adapt well to other forms of transmission. (3) If the writing systems of Chinese and Japanese were not so complex, people would be able to use other means (such as telegraph or digital computer display) to communicate information over long distances.

(6) If Western languages used a writing system like that of Chinese, such digital transmission would probably never have been developed. (9) If there weren't so many individual characters, or if the writing system had a clear correlation between a single symbol and a single sound, the fax would surely not have become so widely used in such a short period of time.

(12) Had this not been the case, the widespread use of fax machines would probably not have happened so quickly.

POSSIBLE NONHYPOTHETICAL PARAPHRASES:

(2) But its use grew so rapidly because certain Asian writing systems didn't adapt well to other forms of transmission. (3) The writing systems of Chinese and Japanese are complex, and people haven't been able to use other means (such as telegraph or digital computer display) to communicate information over long distances.

(6) Western languages don't use a writing system like that of Chinese, and so digital transmission developed. (9) There weren't so many individual characters, nor does the writing system have a clear correlation between a single symbol and a single sound. As a result, the fax became quite widely used in such a short period of time.

(12) The widespread use of fax machines happened so quickly because this was the case.

Exercise 16

Answers will vary. Possible answers include:

1. Otherwise I'd buy you a car; I'd buy you a car, but I don't have a million dollars.
2. Otherwise I'd be in the university; I'd be in the university, but I don't yet speak English perfectly.
3. Otherwise, they wouldn't have enough expertise; Doctors wouldn't have enough expertise, but (for the fact that) they have to spend many years in medical school.
4. Otherwise, she would worry about me; My mother would worry about me, but she doesn't know how I am living now.
5. Otherwise I would still be at home; I would still be at home, but my father is not the leader of my country.
6. Otherwise I would have a bad case of culture shock; I would have a bad case of culture shock, but (for the fact that) I have many good friends.
7. Otherwise everyone would pass it on the first try; Everyone would pass the TOEFL on the first try, but (for the fact that) it is a difficult examination.
8. Otherwise, I wouldn't have written this book; I wouldn't have written this book, but (for the fact that) English isn't an easy language to learn.
9. Otherwise, there wouldn't be so many intensive English programs; There wouldn't be so many intensive English programs in the United States, but (for the fact that) many students come here for university study.
10. Otherwise we would hold the wedding outdoors; We would hold the wedding outdoors, but the weather forecaster has predicted heavy rain for tomorrow afternoon.

Exercise 17

Answers will vary. Possible answers include:

1. Real possibility: If I go home for the next vacation, I'll be sure to bring you a present when I come back.
   Theoretical possibility: If I went home for the next vacation, that would mean that I had already been admitted to the university.
2. Real possibility: If I pass the TOEFL the next time I take it, I will begin my university studies right away.
   Theoretical possibility: If I passed the TOEFL the next time I took it, I would be the happiest person in the world.
3. This is probably a theoretical possibility for all your students: If I became President of my country, I would make my grammar teacher the Minister of Education.
4. Real possibility: If I have eight children, I will probably need to have two jobs to earn enough money.
   Theoretical possibility: If I had eight children, it would probably make me crazy.
5. Real possibility: If I buy a new car within the next three months, I will have to renew my driver's license.
   Theoretical possibility: If I bought a new car in the next three months, I would need to get automobile insurance.
6. Real possibility: If I join the army, I hope I won't have to fight any battles.
   Theoretical possibility: If I joined the army, I would be the oldest recruit in boot camp.
7. Real possibility: If I get sick later today, I won't come to class tomorrow.
   Theoretical possibility: If I got sick later today, I would know that this tuna sandwich has been sitting in the sun too long.
8. Real possibility: If I look for a new place to live, I will consider living with a roommate.
   Theoretical possibility: If I looked for a new place to live, I would start by checking the newspaper want ads.

10. **Real possibility:** If I have free time before class tomorrow, I'll write a letter to my parents.

    Theoretical possibility: If I had free time before class tomorrow, I wouldn't have to do my homework tonight.

Exercise 18

Answers will vary. Possible answers include:

1. Would it be O.K. if I closed the door?
2. Would you mind if I turned down the radio a little bit?/Would it be O.K. if I turned down the radio a little bit?
3. If you ate some more of this pie, it would make the cook happy.
4. I would come to your party if I could.
5. I would take the time to help you if I weren't so busy.

Exercise 19

1. hypothetical event
2. past possibility
3. hypothetical event
4. hypothetical event
5. hypothetical event
6. past possibility

Exercise 20

Answers will vary. Possible answers include:

Nadine Stair wishes that she had been more relaxed.

She wishes she had dared to make more mistakes.

She wishes she had been sillier than she has been.

She wishes she had taken fewer things seriously.

She wishes she had taken more trips.

She wishes she had eaten more ice cream and less beans.

Activities

Activity 1

Either the preparatory list or final essay can be used to check students' understanding and mastery of past hypothetical forms, meaning, and uses.

Activities 2 and 3

These activities can be used to check students' mastery of present and future hypotheticals.

Activities 4 and 5

These can be used for both written and oral practice. Native speakers would likely use hypothetical to discuss the sensitive issues raised in these activities.

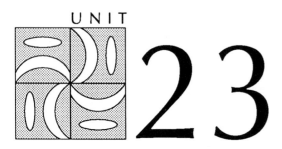

UNIT 23 — Sensory Verbs

Task

You may wish to use the Tasks in this unit and in Unit 24 (Causatives) as follow-up activities for Units 6, 7, and 11 (Infinitives, Gerunds, and Participles). They can also be used as a recycle and review of verb complements, as well as for a specific diagnosis of student knowledge of sensory verbs.

Exercise 1

1. sensory verb: *hear*
   observed action: The birds are singing in that tree.
2. sensory verb: *feel*
   observed action: The wind blows through his hair when he rides his motorcycle.
3. sensory verb: *heard*
   observed action: His voice got louder as he argued with Denise.
4. sensory verb: *saw*
   observed action: The thief picked up the man's briefcase and began to run away.
5. sensory verb: *listened*
   observed action: The old woman complained about her arthritis.
6. sensory verb: *heard*
   observed action: The baby was crying.
7. sensory verb: *watched*
   observed action: Squirrels were gathering nuts for the winter.
8. sensory verb: *smell*
   observed action: Something is burning.

Exercise 2

Answers will vary. Possible answers include:

1. You can hear musicians play music.   You can hear audiences applauding.
2. You can see people skating.   You can watch people fall down.
3. You can smell bread baking.   You can smell good things cooking.
4. You can hear the waves break.   You can hear sea gulls calling.
5. You can see people shopping.   You can see the economy getting worse.
6. You will hear children playing.   You will hear mothers tell their children to be careful.

7. You can hear people practicing sensory verbs.   You can hear students talking about their ideas.
8. You can see people lifting weights.   You can smell people sweating.

Exercise 3

Where both answers are possible, the preferred answer has been indicated by boldface.

1. **ring**/ringing
2. take
3. get/**getting**
4. riding
5. playing
6. leave
7. burning

Exercise 4

Answers will vary slightly. These are possible restatements:

1. (1) Doris observed a man come into the bank. (2) She saw him get in line and hand the teller a piece of paper and a brown bag. (3) She observed the teller putting money in the bag, when a loud alarm began to ring. (4) She saw the guards rush in, but the man had escaped through the side entrance.
2. (1) Mrs. McMartin looked out the window and saw a few children playing on the swings. (2) She saw others climbing on the monkeybars. (3) She watched one little boy running very fast around and around the playground. (4) Suddenly she saw him fall down. (5) She heard him scream in pain. (6) She saw all the other children looking around to see where the noise was coming from. (7) She saw one child running toward her office.
3. (1) During the hurricane, I heard the wind growing louder. (2) I felt the windows and doors shaking. (3) I saw the trees swaying in the garden outside. (4) I heard a tree crash against the house. (5) I heard the sound of breaking glass upstairs. (6) I saw rain pouring through the broken window. (7) I felt a strong wind blowing into the room. (8) I heard the wind howling louder and louder.

Exercise 5

Where both answers are possible, the preferred answer has been indicated by boldface.

1. **ring**/ringing
2. snapping, falling
3. sitting
4. fall/**falling**
5. cry/**crying**
6. drift/**drifting**
7. waiting
8. burning

Activities

Activity 1

This can be done orally or in writing.

Activity 2

This is a good follow-up for the experience in the Task. Responses may need to be structured in order to use this as a testing or diagnostic activity.

Activity 3

This can be used as a cross-cultural observation assignment, by asking students to make a generalization about Americans, and then use their observation to confirm or deny the validity of the generalization.

Activity 4

This can be used as a diagnostic or testing activity.

UNIT 24

Causative Verbs

Task

Students' responses to these questions will indicate whether they understand and can use causative correctly.

What things did your parents make you do that you didn't want to do?

What things did they have you do on a regular basis that you didn't mind doing, but probably wouldn't have done on your own?

What things did they let you do as a reward for good behavior?

Exercise 1

This is an open-ended exercise.

(2) *(a)* — drill instructor; *(b)* — had; *(c)* — him; *(d)* — join all the other new recruits (3) *(a)* — The officers; *(b)* — made; *(c)* — them; *(d)* — stand in the hot sun for several hours (4) *(a)* — They; *(b)* — wouldn't allow; *(c)* — the new recruits; *(d)* — to joke, or talk to each other, or even to move their heads (5) *(a)* — they; *(b)* — had; *(c)* — Army barbers; *(d)* — cut their hair (6) *(a)* — An officer; *(b)* — ordered; *(c)* — Kilroy; *(d)* — to report to a long building (7) *(a)* — The sergeant at Barracks B; *(b)* — had; *(c)* — each man; *(d)* — choose a bunk (8) *(a)* — He; *(b)* — let; *(c)* — them; *(d)* — put their personal possessions in lockers (9) *(a)* — Kilroy; *(b)* — helped; *(c)* — the man in the next bunk; *(d)* — make his bed; *(a)* — that man; *(b)* — helped; *(c)* — Kilroy; *(d)* — to do the same thing (10) *(a)* — The sergeant then; *(b)* — required; *(c)* — the recruits; *(d)* — to sweep the floors and clean the bathrooms

Exercise 2

Answers will vary. Possible answers include:

1. Parents shouldn't make their children go to bed at 6:00, because that's too early.
2. Teachers should help students learn things by themselves, because then they will know how to learn independently.
3. Police shouldn't allow people to break laws, because that will make the society a bad one to live in.
4. Ministers should get rowdy teenagers to come to church so they might become less rowdy.
5. People should have a dentist examine their teeth regularly, because that's a good way to prevent tooth decay or gum disease.
6. Dog owners shouldn't let their pets run around freely, because that might annoy people who don't like dogs.
7. The law should require everyone to pay taxes, because the rich have had too many loopholes for too long.
8. A government shouldn't require all citizens to take drug tests, because this violates individual privacy.

9. A good manager shouldn't allow her employees to do whatever they like, because not everyone is a responsible worker.
10. A good manager should motivate his employees to do their best, because that's the best way to get people to do things.

Exercise 3

let — permit
help — assist
have — employ, hire

get — encourage, convince
make — require

Exercise 4

This can also be used for small-group discussion or structured conversation practice. Answers will vary. Possible answers include:

Teachers should **have** students do homework every night.

Teachers should **help** students guess the meaning of unfamiliar vocabulary.

Teachers should **let** students talk about their lives in class.

Teachers should **get** the students to talk as much as possible.

Exercise 5

This can also be used for small-group discussion or structured conversation practice. Answers will vary. Possible answers include:

- **The government should...**
    make citizens pay/require citizens to pay taxes.
    let them read/allow them to read any books or magazines they wish.
    get them to be/encourage them to be of service to the nation.
    help them meet/assist them to meet national goals.
    have them defend/require them to defend the country.

- **Citizens should...**
    get the government to be/require the government to be responsive to their wishes.
    make the government work/demand the government to work without corruption.
    let the government establish/allow the government to establish national goals.
    have the government maintain/expect the government to maintain law and order.
    help the government provide/assist the government to provide for basic defense.

Exercise 6

1. People aren't allowed to smoke in church.
2. Kilroy was forced to return to the barracks before the movie was over.
3. Everyone who works is required to pay some income taxes.

4. No change possible with *let*
5. No change possible with *have*
6. When I was a child I wasn't allowed to play in the street.

Exercise 7

(1) Once again officers required the recruits to stand in the hot sun... (2) Officers still wouldn't allow them to talk to each other, and wouldn't allow them to sit down. (3) Next they ordered the recruits to go to the medical building. (4) There, dentists examined their teeth and doctors measured their blood pressure. (5) Next was a test of physical endurance, where officers forced the recruits to run three miles in the hot sun. (6) They required recruits who didn't run fast enough to run an extra mile as punishment. (7) By the time the officers allowed Kilroy to return to his bunk at the barracks, he was so tired he could barely walk. (8) As he lay on his bunk he was sorry that the recruiting officer had persuaded him to join the army. (9) That night they allowed the men to write letters to their families, but Kilroy was too tired to do anything but sleep.

Exercise 8

Ways to correct problems may vary.

1. INCORRECT — *got* can't be made passive
   The students were encouraged to do their homework.
   The teachers got the students to do their homework.
2. INCORRECT — *made* doesn't occur with *to*
   The sergeant made the recruits march for several hours.
3. INCORRECT — *had* can't be made passive
   A tailor was employed to shorten my trousers.
   I had a tailor shorten my trousers.
4. INCORRECT — *let* doesn't occur with *to*
   Parents shouldn't let their children watch too much television.
5. INCORRECT — *had* does not occur with *to*
   I had the waiter bring the food.
6. INCORRECT — *encourage* occurs with *to*
   They encouraged all their children to be independent.
7. INCORRECT — *make* doesn't occur with *to*
   Parents should make their children brush their teeth.
8. CORRECT
9. INCORRECT — *made* has the wrong meaning for this sentence
   The babysitter got the children to fall asleep by singing quietly.
10. INCORRECT — *to be* is not correct here
    Kilroy had his hair cut.

Activities

Activity 1

This is best done in small groups.

Activities 2–4

Can be used for writing assignments or discussion topics.

Activity 5

This is most effective when used as an assigned topic for individual speeches. You may wish to include a discussion of effective persuasive techniques in oral presentations.

UNIT 25 Articles in Discourse

Task

You may wish to use the story to evaluate students' use of articles, although probably *all* students at this level will find this unit problematic and challenging.

Exercise 1

This is an open-ended exercise. *D* indicates demonstratives, *P* indicates possessives, *Q* indicates quantifiers, and *A* indicates articles.

<u>A</u> dog is man's best friend. [A] I once had <u>a</u> dog named Poppy. [A] She was <u>a</u> very faithful friend. [A] Every afternoon when I came home, <u>the</u> dog would greet me with kisses and <u>a</u> wagging tail. [A, A] I liked <u>the</u> wagging tail, [A] but I didn't enjoy <u>the</u> kisses very much. [A] Even so, she was always glad to see me, and I was happy to see her too. There was <u>a</u> time in <u>my</u> life [A, P] when I was feeling very lonely. I didn't think I had <u>any</u> friends. [Q] Every day I came home to <u>an</u> empty house [A] with <u>an</u> empty heart. [A] But Poppy was always at <u>the</u> door waiting for me. [A] She seemed to know whenever I was sad or lonely, and at <u>those</u> times [D] she would be extra friendly. <u>One</u> time [Q] she even gave me <u>a</u> "gift": [A] <u>an</u> old bone. [A] Somehow she knew that I was especially sad. She must have thought <u>the</u> bone would cheer me up. [A] <u>Those</u> bad times [D] passed eventually, but they would have been **a lot** [N.B. — *an intensifier, not a noun phrase*] more difficult without <u>my</u> faithful companion, Poppy. [P] She proved to me that <u>a</u> dog really is <u>a</u> wonderful friend. [A, A]

Exercise 2

1. particular
2. generic
3. particular
4. generic
5. generic
6. particular
7. generic
8. particular
9. particular
10. particular
11. generic
12. generic
13. particular
14. generic
15. generic
16. generic

111

Exercise 3

Answers will vary. Possible answers include:

1. *particular:* The store just got a new shipment of bicycles.

   The streets of Beijing are filled with bicycles.

   generic: Bicycles provide cheap and efficient transportation.

   Bicycles were unpopular when I was a boy.

2. *particular:* My Dad just bought a new car.

   We got a new car at the used-car lot.

   generic: A new car will make any man feel five years younger.

   A new car needs to be developed that doesn't use gasoline.

3. *particular:* We felt relieved when we heard the English language being spoken at the hotel.

   We're studying the English language in this class.

   generic: The English language is spoken all over the world.

   Everyone wants to learn the English language.

4. *particular:* I want to come to the party, but I don't have any transportation.

   Can you tell me where I can find transportation to the airport?

   generic: We won't solve our pollution problems until we solve our transportation problems.

   Public transportation is shockingly neglected in California.

5. *particular:* Let's have some tea.

   Please pass the tea.

   generic: Do most people prefer tea or coffee?

   Tea is grown in Asia.

6. *particular:* The store is closed because all the salespeople are on strike.

   If you want to know where the sale items are, you should ask the salespeople over there.

   generic: Salespeople are not well paid in this country.

   Salespeople may not know about the quality of the things they sell.

7. *particular:* There are books all over this desk. Please clean it up.

   The teacher forgot to tell the students to bring their books.

   generic: Books were once so expensive that only very wealthy people could afford to buy them.

   Books always make good Christmas presents.

8. *particular:* Doing this exercise is hard work.

   We really appreciate the hard work you did for us.

   generic: Hard work is good for you.

   No one should be afraid of hard work.

9. *particular:* Let's get some Chinese food for dinner.

   There was a lot of delicious Chinese food at the picnic.

   generic: Chinese food is delicious and healthful.

   Chinese food can probably be found in every country in the world.

10. *particular:* I had some trouble doing this exercise.

    He took a lot of trouble in helping the boy with his homework.

    generic: The TOEFL means trouble for lots of students.

    Many people have trouble deciding what they want to major in at college.

Exercise 4

1. b   2. b   3. c   4. d   5. c

Exercise 5

1. b   2. b   3. b   4. b   5. a   6. b

Exercise 6

1. the
2. a
3. A
4. the
5. some/Ø/the
6. the
7. some/Ø
8. a/the
9. The/a; a; a
10. the; the

Exercise 7

Alternative answers have been indicated.

1. a; Ø; a; a; a; a; The; the/a
2. an; the; the; the
3. some/Ø; The; a; a; the; the
4. Ø; Ø/the; Ø/the; Ø; a; the; Ø/the; Ø/the; the

Exercise 8

Alternative answers have been indicated.

(1) an; an; a/the   (2) a   (3) a   (4) a; Ø   (5) a/the   (6) an   (7) an; a   (8) the; a   (9) a   (10) a   (11) the   (12) Ø/some   (13) Ø/some   (14) the   (15) a; a/the; a/the

Exercise 9

1. c
2. a (a great movie)
3. b (there's only one newspaper in town)
4. d (in the world); d (between Nepal and China)
5. d (we went last year)
6. b (we both know which club)
7. b (we both know which teacher and assignment)
8. d (where I grew up)
9. d (Billy made)
10. b (doctor); d (you've been taking)

Exercise 10

Alternative answers have been indicated.

(1) a (2) a (3) a; an (4) a; the/Ø; Ø (5) Ø; a (6) the (7) the; Ø (8) a; the; a; a (9) the; a; Ø/some (10) an (11) the/some (12) a; a/some (13) a

Exercise 11

Alternative answers have been indicated.

(1) the; a; the (2) the; the (3) a (4) a; a (5) a (7) a (9) Ø (10) the; the (11) the (12) a (14) an; the/a; Ø (15) a (16) Ø; a; Ø (17) Ø; the (18) Ø (20) a; a

Exercise 12

Alternative answers have been indicated.

(1) the; the (2) the (3) a (6) the; the; the; the (7) the (8) the (9) a (10) the (11) the/Ø (12) the; the; the/Ø

Activities

Activities 1 and 2

These two activities work well together, first identifying proverbs, and then creating a "proverb."

Activity 3

Most effective as a small-group activity.

Activities 4 and 5

These are good opportunities to check student writing for errors in form, meaning, or use. You may wish to follow the procedure outlined in that Task of Unit 13 in correcting/discussing students' errors.

Activity 6

Adapts well to use as a paired or small-group fluency circle exercise.

UNIT 26

Demonstratives in Discourse

Task

This task is an open-ended activity. The purpose of this task is to give students an opportunity to observe, analyze, and hypothesize. They therefore should be encouraged to make hypotheses, even ones that may not be correct. They will have opportunities to test the validity of their hypotheses in the rest of the chapter.

Here are some observations (some correct, some not) that students have made on the use of *it,* ***this,*** and ***that*** in this passage:

We use *it* for things and *that* for ideas.

We use *this* for things we just mentioned and *that* for things that we mentioned previously.

That's it and *that's that* have different meanings.

We use *it* for sentences with infinitive complements (It's important to get there early. It's all I can do to keep this office running professionally. It's not easy (to do) when you're only six years old.)

We use *that* for things we don't like. (that nonsense)

Exercise 1

Alternative answers have been provided.

1. these; them
2. them; these/the; the; the; the; This; that
3. It; this/that; It
4. It; the; the/those; they; the; The/that; the
5. this/that; It; It; it; it

Exercise 2

The demonstratives are marked in bold face and what they refer to has been underlined.

2. We hold (**these**) truths to be self-evident, that all men are created equal, and have a right to life, liberty, and the pursuit of happiness.

3. Let me make (**this**) perfectly clear: No new taxes!

4. Frank said that he wanted to leave New York because he was tired of big city life. But I don't think (that) was the real reason for his move to California. The real reason was that his wife wanted to live in a place with warmer winters. At least, (this) is what Stuart told me.

5. (These) soldiers must report immediately to Barracks B: Adams, Collins, and Powell. (These) men have been assigned to patrol duty: Westmoreland and MacArthur. (Those) are your orders, men. Troops dismissed!

6. The causes of the American Civil War were not substantially different from (those) of other wars that have taken place between different regions of any country. (This) is one of the things that can be learned by studying history.

7. The chemical composition of baking soda shares a number of similarities with (that) of any compound containing sodium. (This) is what allows baking soda to enter into a chemical reaction with any compound containing acid, such as (those) found in vinegar or even orange juice.

8. Management techniques of many American companies now tend to resemble (those) used in Japan much more closely than they did a few years ago. (This) is largely attributable to the undeniable success (those) techniques have had in raising worker productivity.

116

Exercise 3

This can be used as an open-ended exercise. Students can compare their answers with the ones listed here and re-evaluate the hypotheses they made in connection with the Task. While in most questions all three are grammatically possible, the *best* answer (based on native speaker responses) has been indicated. In some cases, more than one choice is equally acceptable.

1. that
2. it
3. That/It
4. This/That
5. That
6. that
7. it
8. it
9. It
10. That/This
11. that's
12. That/This

Exercise 4

1. those that help themselves
3. those he likes
4. Those in the stock brokerage business
5. that which is necessary; that which is only desirable
6. Those who can't tell the difference between teal and aquamarine
7. those in charge of that part of the operations

Activities

Like the topic of this unit, the Activities here are all rather open-ended. **Activity 1** is here mostly for fun and should be read aloud to the students once the punctuation has been added. **Activities 2, 3,** and **5** are meant to be done orally. **Activity 4** provides more practice with the concepts introduced in Focus 5.

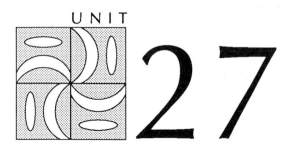

Possessives

Additional Grammar Note:

Pronunciation of -'s or -s' in possessive nouns varies according to the last sound of the word it is added to.		
After voiceless consonants	**After voiced consonants & vowels**	**After sibilants**
it is pronounced /s/:	it is pronounced /z/:	it is pronounced /iz/:
Rick's, Mac's, aunt's, Chip's	Mary's, Sam's, mother's, Joe's	Grace's, church's judge's, Dennis'

Task

Strange things about the picture:

The flowers of the plant are cups and saucers.

The man's shoes are swim fins.

The top of the table appears to be grass.

The legs of the table appear to be human legs.

The fringe of the sofa appears to be fingers.

The shape of the doorknob appears to be a tomato.

The hands of the clock are carrots.

One of the drawers in the dresser looks like a mouth.

The knobs of the TV are happy faces.

The wheels of the child's tricycle are square.

The child's hair looks like snakes.

The dog's tail is very, very long.

The cover of one of the books has a bite taken out of it.

Exercise 1

This is an open-ended exercise. Students can discuss the "meaning" of the possessive structures as part of this exercise or in connection with Focus 3. Many of the structures do not have possessive meanings. You may wish to point out such examples as those in sentences 5, 6, 9, and 10. You can also preview the concept of quantifiers *(one of...)* which is treated in Unit 28.

(1) *(a)* — your   (2) *(c)* — people's   (3) *(d)* — of memory   (4) *(d)* — of items   (5) *(c)* — person's; *(d)* — of numbers   (6) *(c)* — individual's; *(d)* — of unconnected words   (7) *(c)* — people's; *(c)* — hours'   (8) *(c)* — item's   (9) *(d)* — of remembering; *(d)* — of; *(c)* — Shakespeare's; *(d)* — of the poem; *(a)* — their   (10) *(d)* — of information; *(c)* — person's

Exercise 2

1. The results of the investigation
2. Alice's mother's restaurant
3. An individual's ability
4. women's rights
5. The first chapter of the novel
6. The rocket's take-off
7. Elvis Presley's music
8. the discovery of penicillin
9. the children of a very famous American movie star
10. the earth's rotation

Exercise 3

Answers will vary. See Focus 1 for possible answers.

Exercise 4

(1) his roommate Jeff's birthday   (2) Jeff's car   (3) center of the shopping district   (4) stores' parking lots/the parking lots of most stores   (5) doorman of the hotel   (6) the window of one of the stores   (7) the cowboy's hand   (8) the bathroom of their apartment   (9) the front fender of the car   (10) the side of the car   (11) cost of repairs

Exercise 5

Answers will vary. Possible answers include:

1. *What is the most important part of the semester — beginning, end, or middle?*
   The beginning of the semester, because you want the teacher to get a good impression of you right away.
2. *What is your favorite object that belongs to someone else?*
   My favorite object is my brother's car. I wish I had one too.

3. *What is the most important period of history?*

   I think that the present day is the most important period of history, because there have been so many changes in the forms of government and the kinds of economic structures.

4. *What is your favorite piece of music?*

   My favorite piece of music is "Mathis der Mahler" by Paul Hindemith.

Exercise 6

1. *(c)* — of alcohol; *(f)* — individual's
2. *(d)* — of France
3. *(c)* — teacher's
4. *(b)* — the book's
5. *(a)* — days'
6. *(e)* — of short-term memory; *(c)* — of personal importance
7. *(b)* — of the porch
8. *(c)* — Matt's
9. *(d)* — Beethoven's

Exercise 7

This is an open-ended exercise.

(7) *(c)* — Presley's; *(b)* — of the Ed Sullivan Show (8) *(f)* — His; *(x)* — of the screams; *(b/c)* — of his adoring fans (9) *(f/b)* — Presley's; *(x)* — of the objections; *(d)* — of TV broadcasters; *(d/f)* — his (10) *(c)* — America's; *(c)* — of all time (11) *(a)* — of records; *(a)* — of films (12) *(a)* — of screaming, adoring fans

(13) *(f)* — his (14) *(e)* — of; *(f)* — his troubles (15) *(f)* — his (16) *(f)* — His; *(f)* — his; *(f/d)* — friends' *(x)* — of his life (17) *(d)* — of; *(f)* — his own popularity.

(18) *(x)* — of; *(f)* — his death; *(c)* — of Rock and Roll (19) *(a)* — of adoring fans (20) *(d)* — His; *(d)* — Presley's

(22) *(f)* — his; *(d)* — of; *(f)* — his fame *(f)* — his; *(f)* — fans' *(f/b)* — his (24) *(a)* — of letters; *(f/c)* — The King's

Exercise 8

1. *Better to use possessive noun with animate nouns.*

   Elvis Presley's fame spread across America.

2. *Better to use possessive phrase with inanimate nouns.*

   The top **of the table** was covered with newspapers.

3. *O.K.*

   The child of Bambang's classmate was sick with the flu.

4. *The possessive phrase is very long.*

   The barking of the dog of Gladys' well-known next-door neighbor annoyed the entire neighborhood.

5. *Studies is not an animate noun.*

   The results of the scientists' studies indicate that memory is affected by such things as weather and time of day.

6. Memory *is not an animate noun.*
   Investigations **of memory** have shown that the ability of people to remember things declines with age.
7. Rock and Roll *is not an animate noun.*
   The King **of Rock and Roll** died in 1977.
8. Death *is not an animate noun.*
   The circumstances of Elvis' death are somewhat mysterious.

Activities

The Activities in this chapter are all designed as structured conversation activities with the exception of **Activities 2** and **4,** which can be used as a written testing or diagnostic activities. The self-monitoring and correction suggested in **Activity 4** is a useful technique that can be applied to either of the written activities in this unit as well as to any written activity in this book.

UNIT 28

Quantifiers

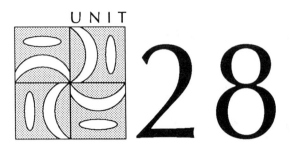

Task

The Task can be done in pairs, small groups, orally, or written. You can elicit additional use of quantifiers by asking specific questions about the graphs, for example: "Do most students study art or literature? No, they don't. Only a few study those subjects. Most students study…," etc. See Exercises 5 and 7 for possible statements that can be made in connection with the statistics presented in these graphs.

Exercise 1

This is an open-ended exercise.

QUESTION (A)

(1) many   (2) few spaces; a substantial number of Americans   (3) not all the doctors   (4) quite a few   (5) all physicians

(6) Most doctors   (7) Every hospital; a few recently graduated medical students   (8) many foreign medical schools   (9) some popular hospitals; a great many applications; each available space   (10) a number of hospitals; only a few   (11) most   (12) A few; some

(13) Many doctors   (14) No doctor; every area; some doctors   (15) Each area

QUESTION (B)

(1) many *(people/experts)*

(4) quite a few *(doctors practicing in the United States)*

(10) only a few *(applications for residency)*

(11) most *(period of training)*

(12) a few, some *(residencies)*

Exercise 2

Answers will vary. Possible answers include:

1. Most doctors study both theoretical and applied topics.
2. Not all doctors are familiar with Western medicine.
3. All doctors try to cure patients as quickly as possible.
4. A few doctors have advanced degrees from the United States.
5. No doctors are children.
6. Many doctors have private practices in addition to working in government-run clinics.

Exercise 3

1. Almost all medical students in the United States already have B.A. degrees.
2. Some students have more than one major.
3. There are a few scholarships for international students.
4. It takes a great deal of money to fund a university education.
5. A few students apply to only one university for admission.
6. Some applicants don't pass the qualifying exams such as TOEFL, GRE, or GMAT.
7. Most international students apply for admission to more than one university.
8. Many students study English before they begin their academic studies.

Exercise 4

1. All *isn't used in negative sentences.*

   Not all doctors **apply** to several hospitals for residency.

2. Some *means a certain group or amount, and can be used with a negative verb. But the second* some *means an unspecified amount, and is not used with negative sentences.*

   Some students don't have **any** trouble passing their exams.

3. Any *is used in questions or negative forms.*

   Other students have **some** trouble, but usually pass on the second time.

4. Much *is used mainly in questions or negative sentences unless the register is elevated (e.g., "You have caused us much consternation.").*

   A medical education requires **a lot of** money.

Exercise 5

Answers will vary. Possible answers include:

1. All foreign students must have a visa; All foreign students must prove they have finances.
2. A great many students use personal and family funds for their education; A great many students study in California, Texas, and Florida.
3. Quite a few students get scholarships from their schools; Quite a few students study business and management.
4. A lot of students study engineering; A lot of students study math or science.
5. Private sponsors provide a little scholarship money; The United States government provides a little money for scholarships.
6. Several states have more than 10,000 foreign students; There are several sources of funds for study other than those in the United States.
7. Some students have undeclared majors; Some students work to finance their education.
8. Students can usually enroll in any college that will accept them; Any foreign student needs a visa to study here.
9. A few students study fine arts; A few states have less than 1,000 foreign students.
10. A great deal of the money foreign students spend comes from personal sources; A great deal of the United States funding for study is provided by colleges and universities.
11. Nevada doesn't have many foreign students; The United States government doesn't supply much money for foreign student scholarships.

Exercise 6

1. few
2. a little
3. a few
4. little
5. few
6. little
7. a few
8. little

Exercise 7

Answers will vary. Possible answers include:

1. Few students get United States government scholarships; Few students come here to study agriculture.
2. Not all states get the same number of foreign students; Not all students have to use personal funds to pay for their education.
3. There is little foreign student demand for agricultural programs; There is little reason to come to the United States to study foreign languages.
4. There are hardly any foreign students in Montana; Hardly any students study agriculture anymore.
5. No student can escape culture shock; No student can study in two states at the same time.

Exercise 8

Alternative possible answers have been provided.

1. Any/every doctor must complete his or her residency within two years.
2. Any/every parent wants his or her children to succeed in life.
3. Peter spends every free weekend at the beach.
4. Each/every person who came to the examination brought a calculator.
5. A wise student takes advantage of every/any opportunity to gain practical experience.

Exercise 9

Answers will vary. Possible answers include:

1. is learning about English grammar; is hoping to pass the TOEFL.
2. has told me to speak as much as possible; has taught me something.
3. will have students of different abilities; is boring.
4. likes homework; wants to fail this class.
5. sleep in class; ignore rude behavior.

Exercise 10

1. both   2. neither; both (of them)   3. either   4. either (of them)

Exercise 11

Answers will vary. Possible answers include:

1. Both Abdul and Chen like to study grammar.
2. Neither student has passed the TOEFL, but both of them hope to by the end of the semester.
3. Chen hopes to go to either Harvard or Duke for his M.B.A.
4. Kasumi doesn't want to marry either of them.

Exercise 12

1. All
2. Any
3. Almost all
4. Most
5. much of
6. A great deal of
7. Some of
8. any of
9. little of
10. No

Exercise 13

Answers will vary. Possible answers include:

1. Yes, they do; All have to pass.
2. Not all pass on the first try; Quite a few don't pass on their first try.
3. Not many are well-trained in non-Western medicine; Only a few are well-trained in non-Western medicine.
4. It takes quite a bit to get a medical education in the United States; It takes a lot to get a medical education in the United States.
5. There's a great deal; There's quite a bit.
6. All have basic first aid training.
7. They usually apply for several; They usually apply for a few.
8. Quite a few study overseas; Many study overseas.
9. Some are enrolled in the United States, but not many.
10. It takes a lot; It takes quite a bit; It takes a great deal.

Exercise 14

1. any
2. few
3. came
4. quite a bit of/a bit of
5. Not all
6. much
7. a lot
8. neither
9. a certain amount of
10. A great deal of

Exercise 15

1. No doctor is allowed to practice without a license.
2. We had a lot of trouble with the examination this morning.
3. A great many traditional medicines are still used in rural areas.

4. *correct*
5. *correct*
6. *correct*
7. Quite a bit of the time that Albert spent in his residency was clinical training.
8. Students usually apply to several universities for admission.
9. *correct*
10. *correct, but awkward:* Most students take their studies seriously.

Activities

Activity 1

If you wish, you can have the students use this information to generate sentences with specific quantifiers such as those listed in Exercises 5 and 7.

Activity 2

This adapts well to the topic of using visual aids in speeches.

Activity 3

Students can be asked to refer to the essay in Exercise 1 as a model of the kind of essay they should write.

Activity 4

This is similar in scope of Activity 2, and works best as an oral presentation.

Activity 5

Students can report in a short essay or speech to the rest of the class.

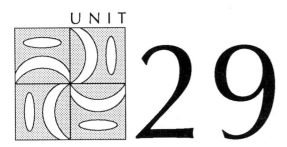

Collective Nouns

Task

If you like to use a lot of small-group work in your classes, you may wish to use this Task early in the semester. You can follow up the group presentations by generating a list of effective techniques and "traps" to avoid that you want small groups to use throughout the course.

Exercise 1

1. a large flock of swallows; this flock; they; The Chamber of Commerce; flocks of tourists
2. Teams of athletes; A team's; it; A team; its; The young, the enthusiastic; the dedicated; them; them
3. A committee; the government; They; their; The press; the public; the committee; its
4. company; the company; The National Theater of the Deaf; they; The troupe; the disabled

Exercise 2

This is an open-ended exercise.

1. <u>The Roman Catholic clergy</u> will resist any attempt to change <u>its</u> position on abortion.

    REASON: Focus on the whole group, not individual members of the group.

2. The victorious <u>team</u> all waved to <u>their</u> supporters while <u>the crowd</u> roared <u>its</u> approval.

    REASON: Team members wave in different ways, the crowd behaved as a single entity.

3. <u>The media is</u> aware of the important role <u>it plays</u> in American presidential elections.

    REASON: An abstract single entity.

4. <u>The herd of sheep</u> bleated nervously to <u>its</u> shepherd as <u>a pack of wolves</u> made <u>its</u> way through the forest.

    REASON: The sheep behaved individually, and the wolves behaved as a group.

5. <u>The military continues</u> to fight further reductions in <u>its</u> funding.

    REASON: Focus on the whole group, not individual members of the group.

6. <u>The middle class is</u> facing a greater tax burden than <u>it has</u> ever faced before.

    REASON: An abstract single entity.

7. <u>A rash of new developments have</u> made a great change on <u>the government's</u> priorities, and <u>it is</u> just beginning to respond to <u>them</u>.

    REASON: The author wants to keep the pronoun reference clear: *developments* — plural; *government* — singular.

Exercise 3

This is an open-ended exercise. The most likely reasons have been indicated.

1. The staff took a vote on what kind of Christmas party **they want. They** decided to rent a hall and hire a band. *(Singular sounds very British.)*
2. The college administration **wants** a basketball team that **is** able to win enough games to place **itself** in the final play-offs. *(The college administration and the team are single entities.)*
3. The rowing crew raised **their** oars as **their** boat crossed the finish line. *("Oars" in plural implies that we will talk about the crew members, since each member has a pair of oars.)*
4. The advanced grammar class never like to turn in **their** homework right after a long vacation. **They** prefer to finish all assignments before **they** leave for vacation. *(It might be preferable for the first sentence since it's the advanced grammar class, rather than "students in the advanced grammar class." However, the following sentences seem more natural with plural forms.)*
5. The crowd showed **its/their** approval by letting out a deafening roar. *(Both are possible.)*
6. The opposition voiced **its** disapproval to the policies the government had released in **their** latest report by more than three dozen speeches in Parliament. *(By making "government" plural, pronoun reference is clearer.)*

Exercise 4

Sentences will vary. Only one example has been provided.

1. *Singular:* The National Assembly has just passed a law making independent thought illegal.
2. *Plural:* The French are not famous for their tolerance or politeness to tourists.
3. *Plural:* The Russians are facing another winter of food shortages and social instability.
4. *Plural:* The Washington Redskins have just won the Superbowl.
5. *Singular:* The government of Brazil is trying unsuccessfully to combat inflation.
6. *Singular:* The Catholic Church opposes the separation of church and state on a number of important social issues.
7. *Plural:* The Chinese are famous for their cooking.
8. *Plural:* The Grateful Dead are popular with aging hippies.
9. *Plural:* The Smith Family are all going to France to visit John.
10. *Plural:* The Simpsons are popular cartoon characters.

Exercise 5

You may wish to have students frame their restatements as rewrites of the full original sentences.

1. *the young* = people who were young
2. *the lonely and the confused* = people who are lonely and confused
3. *the oppressed* = people who are oppressed
4. *the sick* = people who are sick
5. *the underprivileged* = people who are underprivileged

Exercise 6

(1) are   (2) consist   (3) consists   (4) its   (5) were; their   (6) have; they   (7) are   (8) are   (9) them; have; their; they   (10) they   (11) have/their   (12) are   (13) are; are   (14) represents   (15) are; has; its; their

Exercise 7

This is an open-ended exercise.

1. The mayor was followed by <u>a pack of reporters</u> demanding to know whether he was planning to resign. *(The author implies that the reporters acted like wolves or dogs, barking questions and snapping up answers.)*
2. When <u>herds of tourists</u> filled the gallery, John decided to see the exhibition at another time. *(The author implies that the tourists acted like cattle.)*
3. <u>A flock of schoolchildren</u> filled the air with shouting and laughter. *(The author implies that the children acted like birds, hopping and chirping.)*
4. Out of the jungle came <u>a troupe of monkeys</u> which snatched up the food that had been prepared for the picnic. *(The author implies that the monkeys were like actors or acrobats.)*
5. As soon as he stepped out of the limousine, he was surrounded by a <u>swarm of beggars</u> asking for money. *(The author implies that the beggars were like annoying insects.)*

Exercise 8

1. The Supreme Court **has** decided to reverse **its** opinion on that issue.
2. *correct;* **they** *is also possible.*
3. The rich **are** always trying to avoid giving **their** money to pay taxes.
4. The Kremlin **is** trying to restructure the economy of the USSR.
5. The herd of sheep was frightened by a pack of wolves, and **they** bleated nervously in their pen.

Activities

Activity 1

This activity is for fun, not for serious vocabulary development.

Activity 2

Even a few sentences on each topic will allow you to evaluate whether or not students have a working knowledge of collective nouns.

Activity 3

This can be combined with the suggested Task follow-up activity on good practices/strategies for group-work.

Activities 4 and 5

These can be done orally, or as written reports.

Special Problems in Past Time Frame
Choosing Adverbs versus Aspect Markers to Indicate Time Relationships

Task

If you are doing this unit as part of a general review of verb use, you can also have students underline all the verb phrases in the two sample passages. Exercise 5 asks them to identify and explain the uses of past progressive. You can use the example passages for other tenses in Past Time Frame.

Exercise 1

This exercise will hopefully be a review activity for students at this level. There are a variety of ways to review these forms. Students can do the exercise individually or in pairs or groups. It can also be used as a quiz or test of the students' knowledge.

Simple Form	Past tense Form	Past Participle
become	became	become
begin	began	begun
bend	bent	bent
bet	bet	bet
bind	bound	bound
bite	bit	bit
bleed	bled	bled
blow	blew	blown
break	broke	broken
bring	brought	brought
build	built	built
buy	bought	bought
catch	caught	caught
choose	chose	chosen
come	came	come
cost	cost	cost
cut	cut	cut
dig	dug	dug
do	did	done
draw	drew	drawn
drink	drank	drunk

Simple Form	Past tense Form	Past Participle
drive	drove	driven
eat	ate	eaten
fall	fell	fallen
feed	fed	fed
feel	felt	felt
fight	fought	fought
find	found	found
fit	fit	fit
fly	flew	flown
forbid	forbade	forbidden
forget	forgot	forgotten
forgive	forgave	forgiven
freeze	froze	frozen
get	got	gotten
give	gave	given
go	went	gone
grind	ground	ground
grow	grew	grown
hang	hung	hung
have	had	had
hear	heard	heard

Simple Form	Past tense Form	Past Participle
hide	hid	hidden
hit	hit	hit
hold	held	held
hurt	hurt	hurt
keep	kept	kept
know	knew	known
lead	led	led
leave	left	left
lend	lent	lent
let	let	let
make	made	made
mean	meant	meant
meet	met	met
put	put	put
quit	quit	quit
read	read	read
ride	rode	ridden
ring	rang	rung
rise	rose	risen
run	ran	run
say	said	said
see	saw	seen
seek	sought	sought
sell	sold	sold
send	sent	sent
set	set	set
shake	shook	shaken
shine	shone	shone
shoot	shot	shot
shut	shut	shut
sing	sang	sung
sink	sank	sunk

Simple Form	Past tense Form	Past Participle
sit	sat	sat
sleep	slept	slept
slide	slid	slid
speak	spoke	spoken
speed	sped	sped
spend	spent	spent
split	split	split
spread	spread	spread
spring	sprang	sprung
stand	stood	stood
steal	stole	stolen
stick	stuck	stuck
sting	stung	stung
strike	stuck	stricken
swear	swore	sworn
sweep	swept	swept
swim	swam	swum
swing	swang	swung
take	took	taken
teach	taught	taught
tear	tore	torn
tell	told	told
think	thought	thought
throw	threw	thrown
understand	understood	understood
wake	woke	woken
wear	wore	worn
weave	wove	woven
weep	wept	wept
win	won	won
wind	wound	wound
write	wrote	written

Exercise 2

This is an open-ended activity.

1. Order of events: How indicated:
    1. had been   aspect, adverbial (for some time)
    2. had been seen   aspect
    3. had obtained   aspect, adverb (once)
    4. entered   sequence

5. discovered	sequence	
6. had uncovered	aspect	
7. reported	adverb (yesterday)	
8. announced	sequence	
9. may lead	future time (indicated by modal)	

2. **Order of events:**   **How indicated:**

1. had been working	aspect	
2. had been trying	aspect	
3. was	adverbial (at the time of the earthquake)	
4. had gone off	aspect, adverbial (at the moment the earthquake struck)	
5. began to sway	sequence	
6. were screaming	aspect	
7. fell	sequence	
8. were working	aspect	
9. were trying	sequence, aspect	
10. stopped	adverb (before)	
11. ran	sequence	

Exercise 3

This is an open-ended activity. The time relationships between the verbs have also been indicated diagrammatically here, and you may wish to use the diagrams when the exercise is discussed by the whole class.

	first action	second action	how indicated
(1)	had been looking ----------------------------×	broke out	adverb (before), aspect
(2)	reached ×	became ×	sequence
(3)	had been looking ----------------------------×	had	aspect, adverb (now)
(4)	were screaming -----×-----	ordered	aspect
(5)	decided ×	began ×	sequence
(6)	hadn't been invented ----------------------------×	didn't fiddle	aspect
(7)	had not been responsible ×	were never determined ×	aspect
(8)	had been looking for ----------------------------×	provided	aspect
	began ×	take ×	sequence

Exercise 6

This is an open-ended exercise. The past progressive describes actions already happening at the moment of focus (*when* clause), and simple past describes actions that happen after the moment of focus (*when* clause).

Passage 1:

1. He had been (was) studying in the library.
2. He left the library.
3. They were rehearsing.
4. People began crying and all normal activities came to a halt.

Passage 2:

1. He was trying to finish a project that he had been working on.
2. He tried to get out as quickly as possible.
3. They stopped working.
4. People were standing around, wondering what to do.
5. Someone appeared who had a transistor radio.
6. Matt and the dog were sitting outside.
7. He and Matt told each other about their experiences.

Exercise 7

This is an open-ended exercise. In most cases, progressive aspect indicates events already in progress, duration over time, or multiple actions or events. The sentences from the example passages of the Task with past progressive and past perfect progressive verbs have been listed here.

Example 1:

(3) was studying   (6) was conducting   (10) were playing; were trying   (17) were still rehearsing

Example 2:

(3) had been trying   (6) were screaming   (7) were moving   (9) were working   (11) were standing   (14) were both sitting

Exercise 8

(1) links, were looking   (2) believed; connected   (3) sent   (4) investigated   (5) found; made   (6) were exploring; made/were making   (7) were discovered; were looking

Exercise 9

This is an open-ended exercise.

Passage 1:

Moment of Focus	Time Before	How Indicated
1) we left on the trip	we checked the car	adverb (before)
2) we made sure the tires had enough air	we checked the oil	adverb (after)
3) we realized	we hadn't gotten more than a few miles/we had forgotten something/we had left our suitcases	aspect (past perfect)
4) we left without thinking about the contents	we had been worrying so much	aspect and adverb (*so/that*—cause & effect)

Passage 2:

Moment of Focus	Time Before	How Indicated
1) the population was a third smaller	than it had been at	adverbial (By the end of the fourteenth century)
2) It was one of the few times in history	the population had stopped growing/had decreased	aspect
3) This smaller population was caused by repeated outbreaks of Bubonic Plague	that had swept through the continent	aspect
4) the century ended	this had resulted in some fundamental changes	aspect
5) the traditional feudal landlords were forced to intermarry with wealthy merchant families, rather than aristocratic ones.	So many people had died	aspect/adverbial (*so/that*—cause & effect)
6) People were able to become craftsmen and artisans.	who had previously only had the opportunity to make a living as farmers or serfs	aspect
7) the traditional social boundaries were wiped out this created a period of great social mobility and economic change	The Plague had killed so many people that	aspect/adverbial (*so/that*—cause & effect)

Exercise 10

1. wanted; had started
2. went; had/had had
3. stopped moving; tried; had stopped working
4. had grown
5. looked; didn't find; had disappeared
6. announced; had been shot; came
7. went; had left
8. was; hadn't received

Exercise 11

1. had been trying
2. had been looking
3. had caused
4. had kept/had been keeping
5. had been going

Exercise 12

1. had been working; overheard
2. had experienced; was
3. was; had been doing/was doing; decided
4. had been trying; landed
5. got; saw; had left; were standing

Exercise 13

(1) was; served   (2) was, was learning; gave   (3) was; ran; chopped   (4) discovered; had chopped; was   (5) demanded; had chopped   (6) heard; went; told; had done   (7) am; are; know   (8) was; decided; rewarded   (9) happened; read   (10) think

Activities

Activity 1

Students can find an example of the kind of paragraph they should write in the Task in Unit 25. If you have already done that Task, you may want to use one of the other Activities.

Activity 2

This "write-around" activity is for fun. There is not much opportunity to check individual student's mastery of verbs in Past Time Frame.

Activity 3

Students can tell their story orally to the rest of the class.

Activity 4

This topic is more suitable for advanced students or those who have a penchant for philosophical rumination.

UNIT 31

Modals in Past Time Frame

Additional Grammar Notes:
Focus 3

> COULD AND *WAS/WERE ABLE TO* FORM NEGATIVES AND QUESTIONS IN THE SAME WAY AS OTHER ONE-WORD AND PHRASAL MODALS THAT REFER TO PRESENT AND FUTURE TIME FRAME:
>
> (a) When I was a child, I **could** speak excellent French, but **couldn't** speak English.
>
> (b) **Could** you speak any other languages as a child?
>
> Yes, I **could** speak a little Italian.
>
> (c) **Were** you **able to** go to Joan's party?
>
> (d) No, I **wasn't**. But I **was able to** send her a birthday card.

Focus 7

> WOULD AND *USED TO* FORM NEGATIVES AND QUESTIONS IN THE SAME WAY THAT OTHER MODALS DO.

- **They can be used in negative statements:**

    (a) When I was little, I **wouldn't** play anywhere except the park near my house.

    (b) I **didn't use to like** spinach (but now I do). — *Didn't use to* has the additional implication that the opposite is now true.

    (c) I **never** used to like spinach. — *Never* is a more common way to make negative statements about habitual actions.

- **They can be used in questions:**

    (d) **Did** you **use to** smoke?

    (e) **Would** you play Cowboys and Indians when you were little?

    (f) When you were little, **would** you **ever** look under your bed to make sure that there were no monsters hiding there? — *Would* is sometimes used with *ever* in questions about habitual actions to distinguish them from requests. *Did* is also common in such questions.

Task

You may wish to use this as written or in contrast with Activity 1.

Exercise 1

1. a 2. b 3. b 4. a 5. a 6. b

Exercise 2

EXAMPLE 1:

Growing older makes people more careful about their health. That is certainly true for me. I <u>used to smoke</u> *(e)* three packs of cigarettes a day. I <u>would start</u> *(e)* every morning by lighting a cigarette and coughing for five minutes. Whenever I walked up a flight of stairs, I <u>would have to stop</u> *(e, a)* halfway up to take a rest. I knew smoking <u>would eventually do</u> *(f)* serious damage my lungs, but I didn't care. I <u>was going to live</u> *(f)* forever. Besides, I <u>used to think</u> *(e)* that smoking made me look sophisticated and mature.

But then I got married, and I <u>had to think</u> *(a)* about my family. I <u>wasn't going to let</u> *(f)* cigarettes make my wife a widow! I was afraid I <u>wouldn't live</u> *(f)* long enough to see my grandchildren grow up. So I quit smoking and took up running. When I first started, I <u>couldn't run</u> *(d)* more than a few hundred yards before I had to rest. But I knew it <u>would only get</u> *(f)* easier, and the longer I quit smoking, the faster I <u>was able to run</u> *(d)*. Now I <u>can run</u> *(d)* a mile in eight minutes. I'm in much better shape now than I <u>used to be</u> *(e)* when I was younger.

EXAMPLE 2:

Growing older makes people less worried about what other people think. In high school, I <u>used to be</u> *(e)* really shy. I <u>would avoid</u> *(e)* talking to people, and I <u>couldn't express</u> *(d)* my ideas in class without feeling very uncomfortable. I guess I was afraid that people <u>were going to laugh</u> *(f)* at me, or that they <u>would think</u> *(f)* I was strange. In high school, people <u>were supposed to</u> *(c)* "fit in." They <u>weren't allowed to be</u> *(b)* different. So I <u>used to wear</u> *(e)* the same kind of clothes and try to behave the same way as everybody else. I felt I <u>had to be</u> *(a)* "one of the crowd."

Now that I am older, I <u>can stand up</u> *(d)* in front of other people and tell them what I think. I certainly <u>couldn't do</u> *(d)* that in high school. I wear clothes because I like them, not because other people like them. I think I'm much more independent and self-confident than I <u>used to be</u> *(e)* in high school.

Exercise 3

Answers will vary. Possible answers include:

- When I was a child, I was allowed to...
  watch TV late on Friday nights.
  stay over at a friend's house.
  read any kind of book I wanted.
  spend summers at my grandmother's house.

- When I was a child, I wasn't allowed to...
  drink Scotch.
  smoke cigars.
  hang out with unsavory characters.
  drive cars.

Exercise 4

Answers will vary. Possible answers include:

When you were a child, were you allowed to smoke?
  No, I wasn't.
Oh, really? Neither was I.
  Neither Hortensia nor I was allowed to smoke when we were children.

Exercise 5

Answers will vary. Possible answers include:

- When I was a child, I had to...
  make my bed every day.
  clean my room every Saturday.
  help my sister with the dishes.

- When I was a child, I was supposed to...
  do my homework every night, but sometimes I told my parents I didn't have any.
  take care of my little brother, but sometimes I would hide from him so my friends and I could play without him.
  say my prayers every night, but sometimes I fell asleep in front of the TV and didn't say them.

Exercise 6

Answers will vary. See Exercise 4 for an example of the kind of dialogue that might be elicited from this exercise.

Exercise 7

1. specific ability
2. specific ability
3. general ability
4. specific ability
5. general ability
6. specific ability
7. general ability
8. specific ability

Exercise 8

Answers will vary. Possible answers include:

Ten years ago I could ride a bike.

Ten years ago I couldn't speak fluent English.

Ten years ago I couldn't understand American films.

Ten years ago I could play the piano.

Ten years ago I couldn't read and write English.

Ten years ago I could speak a second language.

Ten years ago I could read and write a second language.

Ten years ago I couldn't drive a car.

Ten years ago I couldn't buy alcoholic beverages.

Ten years ago I could run a mile in eight minutes.

Ten years ago I couldn't drive a truck.

Ten years ago I couldn't live independently away from home.

Ten years ago I couldn't attend university classes.

Ten years ago I could swim.

Ten years ago I couldn't play American football.

Ten years ago I couldn't translate things into English.

Exercise 9

This is an open-ended exercise.

1. wasn't able to get; could tell; couldn't do
2. was able to do; couldn't; could solve; could write; was even able to get into; couldn't make

Exercise 10

Answers will vary. Possible answers include:

- When I was a child...

    I didn't believe in ghosts.

    I used to be afraid of the dark.

    I would eat vegetables.

    I would play Cowboys and Indians with my friends.

    I would pretend to be able to fly.

    I wouldn't ride a bicycle, because I was afraid.

    I used to cry when I was hurt.

    I used to spend the night at a friend's house.

    I had a secret hiding place.

    I didn't play with dolls.

    I didn't like going to the doctor.

    I would enjoy going to school.

    I wouldn't obey my older brother.

Exercise 11

Answers will vary. Possible answers include:

When you were a child, did you ever pretend that you could fly?
No, I didn't. But I pretended my bed could fly.
When she was a child, Graziella used to pretend that her bed could fly.

Exercise 12

First Passage:

(2) was going to be   (3) would have   (4) would have; could do; wouldn't have to go   (5) was going to be; was definitely going to have   (6) would have

Second Passage:

(1) was going to spend; was to begin   (2) was going to fly; was about to leave   (3) shouldn't get   (4) might be; would be   (5) could take

Exercise 13

1. UNFULFILLED INTENTION
2. My teacher **wouldn't** postpone the test, so we studied for the entire weekend.
3. The committee organized the refreshments for the party. Mary **would** bring cookies. John **would** take care of beverages.
4. UNFULFILLED INTENTION
5. UNFULFILLED INTENTION
6. I never thought the party **would** be this much fun.
7. UNFULFILLED INTENTION

Exercise 14

In cases where both answers are correct, the most likely answer is listed first.

1. wouldn't/wasn't going to go; would/was going to; she would probably; would want
2. was going to/would be; was going to sing; would/was going to be
3. would go; would/was going to be
4. was going to/would finish; wouldn't/wasn't going to be; would probably be/was probably going to be
5. would cause; would happen; was going to do; would be

Exercise 15

This is an open-ended exercise.

Activities

All the activities in this unit adapt equally well either to spoken discussion/presentation or to written responses. Having the students write on these topics will give you a good opportunity to check their responses for accuracy of form, meaning, and use. You may wish to follow the procedure outlined in the Task for Unit 13 in correcting/discussing students' errors.

Reported Speech

Task

You may want to review some of the things students discussed about proxemics and nonverbal communication before doing this Task. The content of the exercises and activities in Unit 11 deals with these topics. Otherwise, you may want to discuss as a whole class what the pictures tell us about the two people and their relationship before you have students do the assignment. The Task can also be done easily (and successfully) as is.

Exercise 1

1. Denise felt that Peter needed to be more serious about work.
2. Denise was angry that Peter had come to work 15 minutes late for the second time in a month.
3. She complained that Peter was going to leave the office early to see his child perform in a school play.
4. She didn't like the fact that he was always whistling in the office.
5. She was upset that he had made rude comments about her personal life.

Exercise 2

1. Denise said, "I am annoyed that he doesn't always finish projects on time."
2. Denise said, "I am unhappy that he tells too many jokes at staff meetings."
3. Denise said, "I don't like the fact that he refuses to come into the office on Saturdays."
4. Denise said, "I am upset that he is going to miss an important meeting because he has promised to take his children to the circus."
5. Denise said, "I am angry that he constantly allows his personal life to interfere with his work obligations."

Exercise 3

Precise wording of the rewrites will vary, but the necessary changes in verbs and modals have been highlighted.

Mr. Green said that the personnel officer **would** be asked to speak to Peter. **He also said** that if Peter **couldn't** get to the office on time, he **would** just have to take an earlier bus. He **might** not be crazy about getting up at 5:30, but he **would** have to do it if he **wanted** to keep his job. Personnel **wouldn't** talk to Peter about the other problems he **might** be having, though. **Mr. Green suggested that** one of Peter's friends in the office **could** deal with him directly about his lack of responsibility. **Mr. Green thought that** Peter probably **wouldn't** change much, but he **might** be more willing to listen to the complaints if he **could** get the information from someone he **liked** and **respected.**

Exercise 4

1. Yesterday morning Peter said that he was coming to the meeting that afternoon.
2. When I saw Mary last week, she told me that her father might be able to take that letter directly to the Immigration Office later that day.
3. Last week my brother told me that he had already completed all the assignments he had for his classes that week.
4. Two days ago I spoke to the doctor, and he said that the results of my test would be there by the next morning.
5. Yesterday my mother promised me that the next day, when I came there, she would give me some of her delicious fudge.

Exercise 5

(1) The representatives announced, "The rate of violent crime has decreased significantly over the last five months."
(2) They admitted, "There has been a slight increase in thefts and burglaries, and the Department will continue frequent patrols in all neighborhoods."
(3) They predicted, "The budget will be finalized by the end of this week, and the accelerated hiring program may begin as soon as next Wednesday."

Exercise 6

(2) His parents told him, "We found you under a cabbage leaf."
(3) He thought, "That probably isn't true, since there are lots of new babies in my neighborhood and no cabbage plants at all."
(4) He thought, "My parents actually bought my younger sister at the hospital."
(5) He figured, "Hospitals are places that sell babies to any couple that wants one."
(6) His mother said to his father, "You have to be sure/Be sure to pay the bill before this week is over."
(7) He hoped, "Maybe my father will forget to pay and the hospital will decide to take her back and sell her to someone else."
(8) Here is what he found out: Babies are neither bought nor found.

Exercise 7

1. A number of years ago employers used to ask if prospective employees were married or single.
2. They wanted to know if a prospective employee's wife worked outside the home?
3. They often asked prospective employees to tell them how many children they had.
4. They wanted to know if a prospective employee was a Communist.
5. They wanted to know if a prospective employee went to church.
6. They often asked prospective employees to tell them how old they were.
7. They wanted to know why a prospective employee wanted to work for that company.
8. They wanted to know if a prospective employee used drugs.
9. They often asked what a prospective employee's racial background was.
10. They often asked how much experience a prospective employee had.

Questions 1–5 are no longer commonly asked. Questions 6–10 still are.

Exercise 8

Where did you graduate from high school?
Have you ever studied in a college or university?
Have you ever been arrested?
Have you ever needed to borrow money in order to pay off credit card purchases?
How fast can you type?
What kind of experience do you have with computers?
Are you more proficient in COBOL or BASIC?
What companies have you worked for in the past?
What was your previous salary?
Why aren't you still working at your previous job?
Will you voluntarily take a drug test?

Exercise 9

1. Another officer ordered, "Clean the area (for) the next hour."
2. The officers commanded, "Don't talk to each other."
3. Someone said, "Stand at attention until your papers have been processed."
4. Kilroy asked, "Can I go to the bathroom?" But they told him, "No!"
5. The officer said, "Return to your barracks."
6. Several other recruits asked Kilroy, "Would you like to join us in a game of cards?"
7. He told them, "I'm too tired. Would you please not be too noisy, since I want to sleep."

Exercise 10

1. *No change* — timeless truth
2. *No change* — hypothetical statement
3. *No change* — question occurred a very short time ago
4. *No change* — tense change would result in a change of meaning
5. *No change* — hypothetical statement
6. "This morning Peter told me that he **was** still having problems with Denise, but **he was** trying extra hard to get along with her."

Exercise 11

An open-ended exercise.

1. love is blind; he had finally met the woman of his dreams; he still seems single on Saturday nights; people who are in love were supposed to enjoy being together
2. if you know how I can get in touch with Mona; where she is living these days
3. breathing night air was very unhealthy; people should close all windows when they slept, even in the hottest weather
4. No examples of reported speech.
5. a friend of mine had been put in jail for stealing money from her office; she was guilty or not; it could be possible; Denise would do such a thing

Activities

Activity 1

Students can also write a paraphrase of the dialogues that were written in connection with the Task.

Activity 2

This is a good activity to do in connection with cross-cultural discussions on body language and nonverbal communication or with Activity 3 in Unit 23 (Sensory Verbs).

Activity 3

This can be done in written form as a diagnostic. You can give all the students a recording of the same broadcast.

Activity 4

This is for fun, since you won't be able to evaluate individual students' restatements.

Activity 5

This activity can also be used as the topic for small-group discussion.

Activity 6

Have students compare the direct speech patterns of their story with the indirect speech patterns of what they learned.